CROSS-COUNTRY SKIING

CROSS-COUNTRY SKIING

PADDY FIELD
AND TIM WALKER

THE CROWOOD PRESS

First published in 1987 by
The Crowood Press
Ramsbury, Marlborough,
Wiltshire SN8 2HE

British Library Cataloguing in Publication Data

Field, Paddy
  Cross country skiing.
  1. Cross-country skiing
  I. Title II. Walker, Tim
  796.93   GV855.3

  ISBN 1 85223 070 3

Picture Credits

Line illustrations by Vanetta Joffe

Photographs by the authors

Cover photographs courtesy of All-Sport Photographic Ltd

Typeset by Lee Typesetting, Warminster
Printed in Great Britain,
at the University Printing House, Oxford

Contents

Tim Walker is an instructor at the Scottish Sports Council's National Outdoor Training Centre, Glenmore Lodge, Aviemore. He is a Grade 1 BASI instructor and has extensive coaching experience in Great Britain, Canada and Arctic Norway. He also holds the qualifications of Scottish National Ski Council Mountain Ski Leader and Norwegian Professional Skilaere. To date he has represented Great Britain in biathlon, Nordic skiing and Nordic ski mountaineering competitions and at present is Vice-Chairman of the British Ski Federation's Nordic Committee.

I am delighted to see and read this comprehensive all British book, *Cross-Country Skiing*, by Paddy Field and Tim Walker. Both are expert cross-country skiers in their chosen fields and they have created a good blend of general information for the beginner and technical detail for the more advanced skier. Furthermore, they give us excellent material on all the derivatives of cross-country skiing – biathlon, ski orienteering, ski touring – and in doing so open up the vast scope of this magnificent sport.

I hope the British cross-country skiing public enjoy this book as much as I did.

John Leaning
Chairman, Nordic/Biathlon Committee, The British Ski Federation

Wing Commander Paddy Field is a Technical Delegate for the Fédération Internationale de Ski. A former international athlete and coach, he is widely experienced in all aspects of cross-country skiing and has competed in events in North America and Europe. He has held various posts, including Chairman of the London Region Nordic Ski Club, Chairman of the English Ski Council's Nordic Committee, and Secretary of Royal Air Force Nordic Skiing, and was a member of the British Ski Federation's Nordic Committee.

In this long-awaited book, Paddy Field and Tim Walker have applied their extensive experience and expert knowledge of Nordic skiing to the needs of skiers, with specific and very valuable references to the selection of appropriate equipment and safety factors, in addition to the essential techniques of the sport.

This book gives the most up-to-date information in a highly readable and useful form.

John Shedden
Director of Coaching, English Ski Council

Introduction

What is cross-country skiing? This may seem a strange question, yet it is a fact that the mention of skiing often leads people to think almost exclusively of the Alpine variety of the sport, which is so popular with winter sports enthusiasts and which saturates our television screens. However, skiing is a relative newcomer to the Alps, where it was not introduced until the early part of this century. By contrast, skiing has existed as a sport and as a way of life in Scandinavia for several thousand years.

BRIEF HISTORY

Nobody is altogether sure where and when skis were first invented. Some of the early skis which have been found in Norway, Sweden, Finland and Northern Siberia date back at least 4,500 years and are surprisingly sophisticated. Rock carvings showing skiers are widespread throughout the northern regions, and the best known are again thought to be 4,000 years old. Hunting is the recurring theme depicted, and it seems clear that skis were originally designed to enable our forebears to continue their hunting throughout the cold Scandinavian winters.

The widespread use of skis in the Middle Ages is evidenced by two historical events linking the skiing of that era to the sport of the present day. In 1206, the infant King of Norway, Haakon Haakonson, was rescued from his enemies by his bodyguards, the 'Birchlegs', who carried him more than thirty miles at dead of night, and through a midwinter snowstorm, from the Gudbrandsdal near Lillehammer to the safety of the Osterdal at Rena, thus ensuring the survival of the Royal house. The second event occurred in 1522 in Sweden, when the patriot Gustav Vasa, frustrated by the apathy of the Dalcarlians towards their Danish overlords, fled in exile towards Norway. Overtaken at Salen by two skiers sent after him by the townspeople of Mora, he returned to lead his country to independence. These two separate events are remembered in two great modern citizen races, the Birkebeiner-rennet and the Vasaloppet.

Although, across the centuries, there are frequent references to skiing in European literature, it was not until the nineteenth century that the activity began to attract attention outside Scandinavia. Two events then occurred which were to have a dramatic effect on the development of the sport. In 1868, Sondre Norheim travelled to Oslo from his home in the Telemark region of southern Norway, and for the first time demonstrated true control of the ski, particularly in the turns. Norheim can be regarded as the father of the modern ski, for the arched and waisted ski which he invented has scarcely changed in its dimensions to the present day. Twenty years later, in 1888, Friedhof Nansen, the Conservator of the Bergen Museum, crossed the Greenland ice-cap on skis in thirty-nine days. His book, published three years later, brought skiing to the notice of the general public internationally.

Introduction

In 1911 skis were again to play a major part in an event attracting world attention. While Scott struggled bravely on foot to reach the South Pole, Roald Amundsen raced ahead of him with his team who were specially selected for their skiing ability. Amundsen's point man, who led the party for the major part of their expedition, was Olav Bjaaland, who had won the Holmenkollen race in the previous year. It was to him that Amundsen gave the honour of being the first person to stand on the South Pole. In his preparations for the expedition, Scott had been to Finse in Norway where he had learnt to ski, and it was almost certainly his refusal to allow his party to use their new-found skills that led ultimately to their heroic but unnecessary deaths.

When the first Winter Olympic Games were held at Chamonix in 1924, only the Nordic disciplines (jumping and cross-country skiing) were included. At about this time the British in Switzerland were busy developing downhill skiing, which slowly established itself as a quite separate branch of the sport. With the invention first of the tow-bar, and later of the chair-lift, and the introduction of downhill and slalom to the Olympic programme at Garmisch-Partenkirchen in 1936, the breakaway of Alpine skiing was complete.

Recent Developments

Modern cross-country skiing has tended to develop into two separate but entirely compatible activities: ski touring and ski racing, each attracting its own particular brand of devotees. Ski touring is particularly popular in Norway, but is also well suited to the terrain and snow conditions in Britain. Typically practised in untracked snow, carrying a pack and following the tops of the hills above the tree-line, its attractions lie not only in the physical and technical challenge, but also, like hill walking, in the appeal of solitude, the open air and the beauty of the countryside.

Ski racing has different attractions and ranges in scope from the Olympic champion to the humble ski-jogger. Carried out in prepared tracks, it appeals to those who like to expend physical effort in travelling fast and unencumbered. Although many enjoy the hubbub of competition, there are also many recreational skiers who use prepared tracks without involving themselves in the racing scene. In recent years one development of this side of the sport has been the boom in citizen racing, generally over marathon distances, with many of the major races attracting fields of between ten and fifteen thousand skiers. Paralleling the similar growth in road running and marathons, these races provide a stage on which all can take part, regardless of their standard.

One further branch of racing is the biathlon, in which competitors are required to ski carrying a rifle which they must fire on periodic visits to the range during the race. Any shooting penalties incurred are added to the skier's total time to determine the final result. For obvious reasons, this branch of the sport has been almost exclusively the preserve of the military, but increasing opportunities are developing for civilian skiers to take part.

In this book we have tried to look at all these aspects of cross-country skiing as being different parts of one complete unity, just as the fragments of a jigsaw, incomplete in themselves, combine to form the final picture. We start with basics for the beginner, then move on to more advanced modern skiing techniques. We take a look at some essential equipment - the minimum needed to get started – but also cover more sophisticated aids, with advice on preparation and maintenance. Finally, we have included some thoughts on basic fitness and on serious training programmes. We hope that we have provided a book that can be read not only by the novice, but also by the more experienced skier, who can return to dip into it from time to time to reconsider aspects of his technique or training.

Whether you are a novice or an expert skier, we hope that this book will help you to derive the same pleasure from cross-country skiing as we have done over the course of the years.

1 Getting Started

Cross-country skiing is a very natural sport. It owes little to artificiality and can be carried out wherever there are a few centimetres of snow on the ground. It is true that many resorts nowadays spend large sums of money on expensive track-setting equipment, and there are many skiers whose sole experience is of skiing under these manicured conditions. However, there are equally as many whose delight is to wander through virgin snow, or perhaps to follow in the tracks of some other skier who has passed along the same route earlier in the day, or even in the preceding week, if snow conditions have held in the mean time. Neither is the 'right' or 'best' way to ski - it is a matter of personal choice, or, more often, of using the facilities that happen to be available. In neither case, however, should there be any necessity - given the basic essential of snow cover on the ground - to travel to find man-made facilities such as tow-bars or lifts before one can start to ski.

How then should one set about taking part in this exciting sport? Reading this book is a good beginning and should set you on the right road, but you will find us reiterating that nothing can take the place of good personal tuition from a qualified instructor. In the past it has not always been a simple matter to get such instruction, but cross-country skiing is a rapidly expanding activity and it is no longer difficult for the prospective skier to find someone to teach him the essentials of the sport.

What we need then is some snow and some good instruction. Where can we find it?

LOCATION

Assuming that a beginner will fight shy of anything too exotic, there are three major areas of choice: Scandinavia, the Alps, or Scotland. Each has its good points.

Scandinavia

Scandinavia, for most people on the British cross-country skiing scene, means Norway, although Sweden and Finland have an equally long history of skiing and excellent facilities for the sport - neither should be overlooked. However, we will confine ourselves to Norway here. Norway's attractive qualities are the texture of the snow, the beauty of the natural surroundings and the vast knowledge of skiing that is clearly evident in almost every Norwegian, and certainly in those who have achieved the status of an instructor. Skiing in Norway is akin to a religion, and after a while you will begin to give credence to the myth that Norwegian babies are born with skis on their feet.

While Norway is looked on as a skiing paradise by some, it does have its disadvantages. For a start, it can be very cold, and whilst cold weather does have some things in its favour, such as eliminating the difficulties inherent in waxing skis at warmer temperatures, not every holiday-maker wants to risk numb fingers, or even

Fig 1   Scandinavia is noted for its excellent snow conditions and long season. In this picture two members of the British Ladies' Squad take advantage of deep powder snow for some November training at Nordseter.

frost-bite, as he learns to ski. Norway is also expensive, both in terms of travel which can eat into precious holiday time, and money, with high prices for many items in the shops, particularly alcohol. Holiday 'extras' can therefore place a considerable extra burden on a tight budget, particularly since the early winter days are short and you will probably spend a lot of your time inside your hotel.

The Alps

An alternative option to Norway is to try the Alps. Well known already for their down-hill skiing facilities, France, Germany, Austria, Switzerland and Italy have made great attempts to woo the cross-country skier during the past decade. The advantages of the Alpine countries are that they are relatively cheap and easy to reach, being well served by the majority of major travel firms, whose bulk bookings keep prices down.

The Alps tend to be warmer than Scandinavia, which brings the benefit of a sun-tan, but also poses problems for waxing skis and may affect the reliability and condition of the snow. Early in the season, say until mid-January, snow in the Alps can be very unreliable, and if booking ahead it is as well to ensure that the resort

5

Fig 2   *In the Alps snow cover is less reliable. December sunshine forces these skiers in the Dachstein area of Austria to pick their way carefully. Molehills just in front of the leading skier and tyre tracks in the field behind show just how thin the blanket of snow actually is.*

chosen lies at no less than 1,000m (3,280ft) above sea-level. Late in the season, it is a frequent Alpine phenomenon for the snow to melt in the afternoon and freeze again at night, leaving a glaze of ice which does nothing to improve the confidence of the novice skier.

In Scandinavia it is latitude that is the guarantee of good snow, whereas in the Alps altitude fulfils the same function. The vast majority of Alpine cross-country skiing is, however, on prepared tracks, and the steepness of the mountain sides confines the trails to the bottom of the valleys and the lower slopes. The general tendency is therefore for cross-country courses to be undemanding, although this is a rather sweeping generalisation and the experienced (or unwary) skier can soon find terrain to test the most advanced skills in his repertoire. Alpine resorts and villages, long used to the winter tourist industry, have in most cases excellent hotel and *après-ski* facilities and, as a general rule, prices are considerably lower than in the Scandinavian countries.

Scotland

The final possibility is Scotland. There are, of course, many occasions when the weather provides opportunities to ski in

*Fig 3   In good years, the skiing in Scotland can be excellent. The
exceptional winter of 1985-86 saw large numbers of skiers out on
the tracks in the Clashindarroch Forest.*

other parts of the British Isles, but the
latitude and mountains of Scotland give the
only realistic guarantee of satisfactory
snow cover. At its best, Scottish skiing
matches the best that can be found
anywhere in Europe and the facilities are
improving year by year. In the Aviemore
area, there are a number of well-established firms of cross-country skiing
instructors who run courses and classes in
the Cairngorms through a surprisingly long
season. Other areas too are opening up in
response to the increasing demand. The
Forestry Commission is developing an
extensive cross-country area in the Clashindarroch Forest near Huntly, whilst
Glen Isla also has a reputation as a leading
cross-country centre. These areas all
boast tracks along forest paths when the

snow is lying at low level, but it is also
possible - particularly in the Cairngorms -
to ski-tour at higher level and above the
tree-line.

The advantages of Scotland for the
British skier are ease of access (the overnight train from Euston arrives at Aviemore
in the early morning, permitting a full day's
skiing) and no language problems. The
instruction too is geared to the level of
British skiing, which may not necessarily
be the case in Scandinavian or Alpine
resorts. On the other side of the coin, the
snow cannot always be relied upon, and if
you are travelling from the south of
England, the costs are no less than a
package skiing holiday in the Alps. It is,
however, our belief that the developing
facilities in Scotland will expand still further

as general interest in the sport increases, and that the potential of the area, which is still relatively untapped, will be progressively exploited to provide ever-increasing amenities for skiers who live within easy travelling distance.

Travel and Accommodation

Having made the choice of where to ski, the next problem is how to get there. The obvious answer is the holiday package. Many of the traditionally Alpine-only winter sports travel firms now include cross-country skiing in their brochures, although details are often hidden in paragraphs with headings such as 'For those who don't ski'. You may wonder just how much the writers of these brochures know of the history of skiing!

For those thinking of setting out on their first cross-country skiing holiday, it is perhaps safer to stick with the well-established specialists in the cross-country field, who have built up their expertise and their clientele over many seasons of business. These firms will normally operate their holidays in groups of about twelve, with a party leader who is always an experienced skier, but who may or may not be a qualified instructor.

An alternative approach is to make your travel (and possibly accommodation) arrangements yourself and to go to a resort offering a course of basic lessons. This is a good solution to the problem, but involves rather more organisation and may leave you with the difficulty of trying to cope with an instructor who is much more at home in his native tongue than he is in English. Local instruction is normally of a good standard, but it is as well to check beforehand that English-speaking instructors are available.

EQUIPMENT

Having made your travel arrangements, the next problem is the provision of the necessary equipment. At the higher levels, and particularly in the field of competitive race skiing, the sport has become extremely dependent on equipment and skiers can spend vast sums of money on specialised items of kit, either to keep up with fashion or in the hope that they will save precious seconds during the next competitive event. This subject will be dealt with in more detail in the following chapters. Here it is only necessary to mention that for the beginner, cross-country is a very cheap sport, requiring no more than skis and bindings, and a pair of poles and boots. There is no need to launch into the buying of fancy suits or expensive, specialised skis until you have decided whether you really do like the sport and which particular avenue, such as touring, citizen racing or telemarking, you wish to follow.

In the first instance then, a tracksuit or a pair of walking breeches and long socks will suit your purpose admirably. With a cagoule to keep out the wind and falling snow, a pair of waterproof gloves, and a hat to protect the head against heat loss and the elements, you are ready to go.

As for the essential tools of the trade – skis, boots and bindings – these are normally readily available for hire at any recognised resort, and, being cheaper than the Alpine variety, the hire cost adds little to the overall expense of a holiday. It is therefore prudent for the absolute beginner to hire, rather than to face the possibility of wasting money by buying unsuitable equipment.

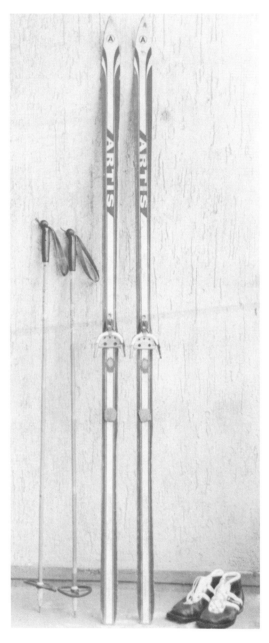

Fig 4 *A cheap and simple package for the novice cross-country skier. A pair of light touring skis, bamboo poles, boots and 75mm bindings.*

Buying Equipment

There will, of course, be those who are already convinced that cross-country skiing is their scene and who, in spite of this advice, wish to buy their own equipment at the outset. For them, two main options are open; they can buy in Britain or they can buy abroad. If buying in Britain, our advice is without question to buy from one of the several specialist cross-country equipment shops, whose reputation depends upon the advice and the service that they offer to their customers. There are numerous stockists of Alpine equipment who purport also to deal in cross-country skis. The quality of advice in these establishments, in our experience, varies from a reasonable knowledge of the subject to almost total ignorance. In many cases, the aim will be to achieve a sale rather than to match the customer to the skis that suit his needs. We repeat our advice to stick with the specialists for informed and objective advice.

The advantage of buying abroad is that there will almost certainly be a shop in the resort in which you are staying whose turnover will make it possible to stock a much wider range of kit than all but a few specialists are able to do in Britain. This, in turn, makes it easier for the salesman, who is likely to have a deep interest in and knowledge of the sport, to find a pair of skis which are not only the right type, but which also match the physical characteristics (height and weight) of the skier and, just as importantly, suit his budget.

If you are fortunate enough to be skiing in March, you may well find that you have hit the end of season sales, when the winter equipment is cleared out and the shop stocks up with summer kit. You may be able to pick up what you need at a real bargain price. This course of action is not to be recommended if fashion is more important to you than price. Ski manufacturers, like car producers, change the styling of their skis and clothing every year, and you can quickly be left behind in the fashion stakes. However, if your budget is a more important consideration you might do well to hunt around. Skis can sometimes be found for as little as thirty per cent of the price they commanded during the height of the season.

INSTRUCTION

If you are a beginner, it is wisest, of course, to ensure that you are properly taught from the very start, and this can only be done by attending classes run by qualified instructors. Most European resorts have qualified instructors, and there is now a growing number of clubs throughout England and Scotland which arrange basic instruction for their club members. Details of affiliated Nordic clubs can be obtained by writing to the English Ski Council or to the Scottish National Ski Council, as appropriate (*see* Useful Addresses). Before starting a series of courses, it is useful to ask if the person taking the class holds a British Association of Ski Instructors (BASI) Nordic Licence. The licence is held by an increasing number of ski instructors in the British Isles and ensures a high level of teaching proficiency. However, whilst a BASI award is a guarantee of competence, it does not imply that unqualified skiers should not show others the basics. In the absence of a qualified instructor, advice and guidance from an experienced skier is certainly the next best thing.

Occasionally you may meet skiers who are self-taught, having perhaps read an instruction manual and then put on their skis to try things out in practice. All too often the results are self-evident, the bad habits becoming ingrained and difficult to eradicate under instruction at a later stage. The moral is clear; time spent at the beginning under competent instructors is never wasted.

ETIQUETTE

You have now reached the stage where you have selected your ski area, decided whether to hire or buy equipment and have

Fig 5   Cross-country skiers must respect trail-marking signs. Some show direction and the distance covered.

Fig 6 Some trail-marking signs warn people against walking on the course or any particular local prohibitions, such as dogs on the track or the use of the skating technique (Siitonenschritt).

arranged a course of lessons. Soon you will be ready to explore the trails that are marked and ready for you all over Europe, or to venture on to the untracked snow in the mountains of Scotland. However, before you set out, it might be as well for us to remind you of the etiquette of the ski trail. A sound knowledge of these internationally agreed rules will help to prevent those unpleasant and unnecessary altercations that unfortunately do occur from time to time, even in the friendly world of cross-country skiing. The code is based on common sense and consideration for others; keeping to it adds to everybody's overall enjoyment of the sport.

Code of Conduct

1. *Respect for others*. A cross-country skier must ski in such a manner that he does not endanger or prejudice the progress of others.
2. *Respect for signs*. Trail marking signs must be respected on any trail where one direction is indicated. Skiers should proceed only in the direction indicated.
3. *Choice of tracks*. On cross-country trails with more than one cut track, skiers should choose the right-hand track. Skiers in groups must keep in the right track, behind each other.
4. *Overtaking*. A skier ahead is not obliged to give way to an overtaking skier, but should allow a faster skier to pass

whenever he judges it possible. A skier is permitted to overtake and pass another skier to the left or right, either in a free track or outside the tracks.

5. *Encounter.* Cross-country skiers meeting while skiing in opposite directions should keep to their right. A climbing skier should give way to a descending skier.

6. *Poles.* A cross-country skier should make the utmost effort to keep his poles close to his body whenever near another skier.

7. *Control of speed.* A cross-country skier, especially going downhill, should always adapt his speed to his personal ability, the prevailing terrain and visibility, and to the traffic on the course. Every skier should keep a safe distance from the skiers ahead. As a last resort, an intentional fall should be used to avoid collision.

8. *Keeping the trails clear.* A skier who stops must leave the track. In case of a fall, he should clear the track without delay.

9. *Accidents.* In the case of an accident, everyone should render assistance.

10. *Identification.* All skiers at the scene of an accident, whether witnesses, responsible parties or not, should establish their identity.

2 Basic Techniques

INTRODUCTION

The basic and advanced techniques explained here and in Chapter 3 are designed to be used as an *aide-mémoire*. You are not encouraged to attempt to teach yourself these manoeuvres. Hours of frustration can be avoided by learning these techniques under the guidance of a qualified instructor. Once mastered, they can then be perfected by yourself or with family and friends in your own time. We would stress the importance of careful assessment of snow conditions and terrain before attempting any practice. So often we see skiers struggling to perfect a technique on terrain on which even an expert would have difficulty. A brief description of suitable terrain is given with each technique.

Remember, Nordic skiing involves more muscle groups than almost any other sport, and it is therefore essential that a thorough warm-up of stretching and static exercises is undertaken before starting to ski.

THE TECHNIQUES

Putting on Skis

Ideal terrain: flat. Place the skis side by side on the snow, about fifteen centimetres (six inches) apart. Clear any snow or ice from the binding and sole of the boot. Locate the toe of the boot into the binding and secure. If your skis are fitted with 75mm (3in) Nordic norm bindings, then there is a left and right ski. This will normally be indicated on the binding, either by the words *left* (L) and *right* (R), or more often by the outline of a left or right foot.

If the terrain is sloping, make sure that the skis are placed across the 'fall line' (the steepest, most direct way down the hill).

Alternate Ski Lift

Ideal terrain: flat. A useful exercise for checking that the boot is located correctly in the binding, and also as a familiarisation and warm-up exercise. Using the ski sticks for support, transfer all your body weight on to one ski, then lift the unweighted ski. Practise this on alternate skis and then try it without using the ski sticks for support.

Falling and Getting up

Ideal terrain: flat. Undoubtedly the technique in which you will become most proficient. When you sense that you are about to fall, always try to fall backwards and to one side, so that the most padded area of your anatomy takes the brunt of the fall. To get up again, make sure that your skis are alongside each other. Using your hands or ski sticks as a prop, transfer your body weight over the centre of the skis and stand up. If you have fallen on a slope, make sure your skis are across the fall line and on the downhill side of you before standing up.

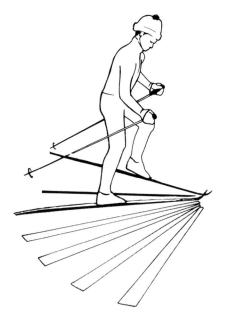

Fig 7   Star turn.

Star Turns *(Fig 7)*

Ideal terrain: flat. Keeping the tips of the skis in roughly the same position, lift alternate heels of the skis, stepping in small steps until you have turned through 360 degrees. You will notice the star pattern left in the snow – hence the name 'star turn'. Practice this in both clockwise and anti-clockwise directions.

Now try a star turn stepping the tips of the skis around while keeping the heels of the skis stationary.

Side-step *(Fig 8)*

Ideal terrain: flat. Using the ski sticks for support, transfer the body weight on to one ski, lift the unweighted ski and take a short step sideways. Transfer the body weight on to that ski and step the other ski in towards

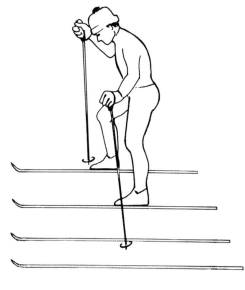

Fig 8   Side-step.

it. The ski sticks are moved together after each step. Whether side-stepping up or downhill, angle the skis in towards the slope, so as to create an edge and platform which will hold the ski.

Two-phase Walk *(Fig 9)*

Ideal terrain: flat. We now move on to the basis of nordic skiing technique. Two-phase (formerly known as diagonal gait) is an extension of our walking gait. Using alternate ski sticks for support, step forward and walk as normally as you can: right arm and left leg forward; left arm and right leg forward. After just a few minutes you will discover that because your body weight is spread over the whole length of the ski, you are not sinking into the snow as much as you were on foot and therefore you are expending less energy.

At this stage you have learnt to walk on the skis, turn the skis using a star turn and

Fig 9   Two-phase walk.

side-step up and downhill, so we would suggest a short tour of a kilometre or so (about three-quarters of a mile) on relatively flat ground.

Two-phase Glide
(Fig 10)

Ideal terrain: prepared track about fifty metres (fifty-five yards) long. We should now look in detail at each of the following component parts of the two-phase action, leg action kick and glide, weight transfer, and arm action.

As the legs pass each other in the two-phase action, there is an initiation of a kick down and back on one ski, followed by a weight transfer and glide on to what has now become the leading ski. With practice the kick will become stronger and, as your balance improves, so you will be able to glide out on the leading ski.

Arm Action

Although arms and ski sticks are used more as outriggers for support in the early learning stages of Nordic skiing, as balance improves the arms are used more effectively in conjunction with the leg kick action to power you forward. The ski stick is placed roughly in line with the binding of the opposite ski, and pressure is then applied down and back through the ski stick. The stronger you are in the upper body, the greater the power and thrust through your ski sticks. A lack of co-ordination between arm and leg action is undoubtedly the most common fault with people learning to ski, but analysis by yourself and comment by others will soon lead to a well co-ordinated action.

Each of us develops a slightly different two-phase action, depending on our build

Fig 10   Two-phase glide.

Fig 11   Double pole

and strength. However, once the action becomes flowing and efficient, it is truly a most graceful technique.

Double Pole (*Fig 11*)

Ideal terrain: prepared track sloping slightly downhill. Standing with skis in the tracks beside each other, place the ski sticks at a full arm's length in front of you. Now bending forward from the waist, push down and back. Stay down low until you sense the skis slowing, then straighten upper body and double pole yourself forward again.

This double pole technique is used to maintain speed when the skis are running well or when the terrain is sloping gently downhill.

Diagonal Side-Step (*Fig 12*)

Ideal terrain: moderately steep hills. We all know that if the terrain permits it, it is easier to take a diagonal line when climbing uphill, rather than to go straight up. With the diagonal side-step we combine the techniques of two-phase and side-step, stepping uphill and forward at the same time.

Herringbone (*Fig 13*)

Ideal terrain: moderately steep. You will discover that when climbing slopes using the two-phase action you will only get so far before your skis start to slip backwards. When that happens, it is time to start using the herringbone technique. The action is still two-phase, but the leading ski is placed

Fig 12   Diagonal side-step.

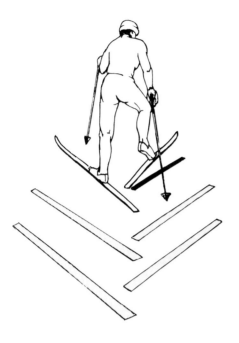

Fig 13   Herringbone.

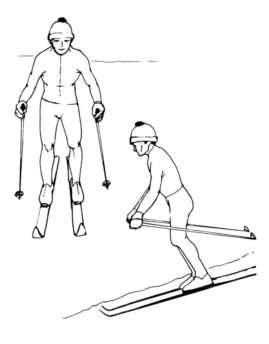

Fig 14   Direct descent.

forward and out to the side to prevent backslip. At this stage the ski sticks are used more to prevent backslip than for propulsion.

Direct Descent (Fig 14)

Ideal terrain: a gentle slope with a platform to start and a good safe run out to stop. The body weight is kept directly over the centre of the skis with the knees slightly bent. Arms are held forward and apart, with the hands slightly forward of the hips. Once the correct position has been found, constant practice will give you the essential ability to stand confidently and relaxed on your skis when travelling downhill.

Traverse Downhill (Fig 15)

Ideal terrain: moderate slope with a safe run out. The angle of traversing line selected will determine the speed at which you travel, so you should select a shallow line to start. Once the traversing technique is mastered, it will be possible to descend moderately steep slopes safely and under control. Standing with your skis across the slope, slide the upper ski forward several centimetres. Now the angle set by the ski tips is followed through the knees, hips, shoulders and arms. Body weight is kept over the centre of the ski, with the majority of the weight on the lower ski. Now select a shallow traversing line, give yourself a push with the ski sticks to start and maintain the traversing position throughout, stepping the tips of your skis uphill to stop at the end of the traverse.

Fig 15   Traverse downhill.

Kick Turns (Fig 16)

Ideal terrain: flat to start with, and then a moderately steep slope. At the end of the traverse the easiest way to turn and select a new traverse line is to use the kick turn. With your skis across the fall line, turn your upper body to face downhill, and at the same time place the ski sticks at full arm's length - one forward and one back on the uphill side of your skis. Now commit all of your body weight on to the uphill ski, rest on your ski sticks, and then kick forward, lifting the lower, unweighted ski; turn it through 180 degrees, placing it parallel with the upper ski. Now commit all of your body weight to that ski, and lift the upper ski, bringing the stick round for support at the same time.

Snow-plough Glide (Fig 17)

Ideal terrain: moderate slope with a safe run out. Using your ski sticks for support in front of you, step your skis around into a fall line. Your sticks are positioned in front of you at full arm's length to stop you sliding downhill. Now, keeping the ski tips in the same position as for direct descent, step the heels of the skis out several centimetres, forming a wedge shape. Weight is still over the centre of the skis and the skis are flat on the snow. Knees and ankles are flexed forward. Holding that position, release the ski sticks and you will glide slowly down the fall line.

Snow-plough Brake (Fig 18)

Ideal terrain: moderate slope with a safe run out. Starting as for the snow-plough glide, the heels of the skis are pushed wider apart, forcing a broader wedge shape. Now experiment, sliding downhill with differing widths of wedge. You will find that the broader the wedge, the slower you glide, and when the heels of the skis are at their widest you will glide to a halt.

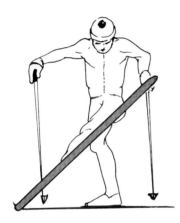
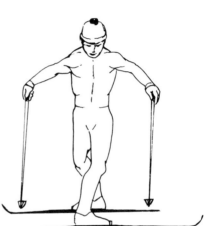

Fig 16   Kick turn.

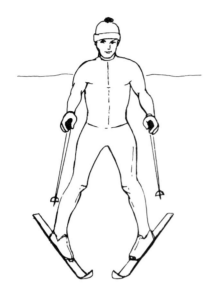

Fig 17   Snow-plough glide.

Fig 18   Snow-plough brake.

Snow-plough Brake (Single Leg)

When skiing downhill in prepared tracks, a single leg snow-plough brake is useful to control your speed. Just lift one ski out of the track and use a half snow-plough braking action.

Snow-plough Turns (Fig 19)

Ideal terrain: moderately steep slope with a safe run out. With the snow-plough glide and brake, the body weight is evenly distributed between the skis. If more pressure is applied on one ski during the glide or braking snow-plough, your skis will begin to turn.

From the gliding snow-plough position, make a positive, slow downsink application of pressure on to one ski, say the right ski, and at the same time steer the knee into the turn. The skis will cross the fall line, and will eventually slow and stop. Now try the opposite side. You will probably find that you have a favourite side where turning comes more easily.

Having mastered snow-plough turns to the left and right, the next step is to link the turns together. Once your skis have crossed the fall line, you should release the pressure from the turning ski and apply pressure to the other ski.

Stem Turns (Fig 20)

Ideal Terrain: a moderately steep, prepared slope. The stem turn is most useful when skiing in difficult or crusty snow. From the traverse position, the unweighted, uphill ski is stemmed out and then pressure is applied, combined with knee steering, to bring the skis through the fall line. Once in the new traverse line, the uphill ski is slid or lifted in parallel to the lower ski.

Fig 19   Snow-plough turns.

Fig 20   Stem turns.

3 Advanced Techniques

Two-phase Uphill (*Fig 21*)

Ideal terrain: flat, gradually increasing to a moderately steep slope, and easing off to become flat again. The two-phase technique adjustments made for climbing uphill will depend largely on the amount of grip you are getting from the wax. On gradually increasing steepness, you will feel when you are about to lose traction. When this happens, a lowering of the body weight over the centre of the ski, and a gradually increased tempo, will restore grip. At this time, the arms and ski sticks come into play, preventing further back-slip. If the slope continues to steepen, and

traction is lost again, then the herringbone or uphill tacking can be used.

Tacking

Ideal terrain: flat, gradually increasing to a moderately steep slope, and easing off to become flat again. Skiing uphill is bound to sap energy reserves and, as with hill walking, it is much easier to make a series of tacks across the slope rather than a direct ascent. As long as the slope is wide enough, exactly the same can be done on skis. The two-phase action is used, but the ski sticks are used slightly more for support. At the end of each tack, the skis

Fig 21   Two-phase uphill.

can be stepped around uphill without a change of tempo. As the uphill ski is stepped around, support is given from the opposite arm and ski stick until the new tacking line is reached. Practise on gradually steepening terrain.

Double Pole with Leg Kick
(*Fig 22*)

Ideal terrain: flat. Occasionally you will find that the terrain and the way in which your skis are running is between two-phase and double pole and then the hybrid of double

Fig 22   *Double pole with leg kick.*

Fig 23   Step turns.

pole with leg kick can be used. The single leg kick is exactly the same as in two-phase, and the initiation comes as the arms swing forward after a double pole. As the hands pass the thighs, a single leg kick down and back is introduced. You will find that you have a favourite side or leg, but as you master the technique you should be able to alternate.

Step Turns Downhill (*Fig 23*)

Ideal terrain: gentle downhill with a good run out. One of the most useful techniques for Nordic skiing, is used for changing direction in difficult snow conditions, for example breakable crust or wet, heavy, newly fallen snow. Stepping the tips of the ski around in short steps thirty centimetres (twelve inches) or so long, a total weight transfer has to take place if you are to

maintain your balance. The steps are made quickly - a useful analogy would be a cat on a hot tin roof.

Side Slipping (*Fig 24*)

Ideal terrain: a moderately steep slope. Side slipping is an exercise in edge control. Using your ski sticks for support, stand with your skis together and across the fall line. Standing up straight, you will notice that the ski edges closest to the hill are cutting into the snow. Now slowly roll your knees and ankles out until the skis start to flatten on to the snow. As this happens, so your skis will start to side slip down the fall line. Practise this, still using your ski sticks for support, until you feel confident enough to side slip without the ski sticks. You will notice that if your body weight is not central over the skis, either the ski tips or

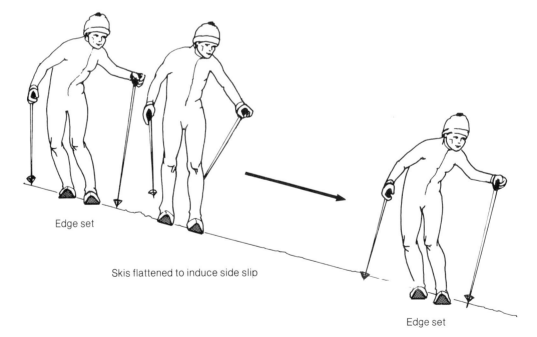

Edge set

Skis flattened to induce side slip

Edge set

Fig 24   Side slipping.

heels will tend to break away.

Forward traversing side slip is a combination of the traversing and side slipping techniques, and can be used for losing height or slowing the skis from the traversing position.

Basic Swing *(Fig 25)*

Ideal terrain: moderately pisted slope. Leading on from linked snow-plough turns, the basic swing is executed in the following way: from a gliding snow-plough, pressure is applied to the inside edge of the outer ski; at the same time, steer with the knee into the turn. The inner ski remains flat on the snow and slides towards the outer ski whilst crossing the fall line. Both skis slide parallel out of the turn. It is important that an open and wide stance is maintained throughout the basic swing, with emphasis on unweighting (taking pressure off the skis) and pressure application.

Swing to the Hill *(Fig 26)*

Ideal terrain: a moderately steep slope. 'Swing to the Hill' is a method of stopping, and a useful build-up to the parallel turn. Starting from the traverse position, with reasonable momentum, initiate the swing to the hill by an upwards motion, followed by a downsink, with a weighting of the inside edge of the outer ski and a steering action with the feet and knees. Continued practice will enable you to attempt this directly from the fall line.

Parallel Turns *(Fig 27)*

Ideal terrain: a moderately steep slope, using small bumps to help turning. A parallel turn is a basic swing with the gliding snow-plough eliminated. It is

necessary to gain momentum before attempting a parallel turn. Once under way, with the skis running parallel and close to the fall line, apply pressure to the inside edge of the turning ski, at the same time steering into the turn with the knees and feet.

Telemark *(Fig 28)*

Ideal terrain: a gentle slope, well pisted. This is the traditional turn for off-piste skiing in difficult or deep snow conditions. Slide one ski forward, and lower your body, with the majority of your weight on the leading ski. If the leading ski is the left one, steer over to the right with the left knee, banking your body slightly over to the left. Arms and hands are held low, so as to lower the centre of gravity and improve stability. The skis are slid back together combined with an upwards motion to finish the turn.

Skating *(Figs 29 to 32)*

Ideal terrain: firm snow, frozen lakes or lochs, or any smooth, well-pisted track. Although skating has been part of the Nordic skiers' repertoire for many years, it has recently been developed to the extent that remarkable speeds can now be achieved using skis, boots and poles designed specifically for the purpose. Training for skating in competitions is specific, and requires considerable strength. Here we are concerned with the recreational skier or tourer who will use skating only when snow conditions permit.

The skating technique is basically as for ice skating, starting with a commitment of all body weight on to one ski. The weighted ski is then edged inwards to form a platform from which to push. All the body

Fig 25   Basic swing.

Fig 26   Swing to the hill.

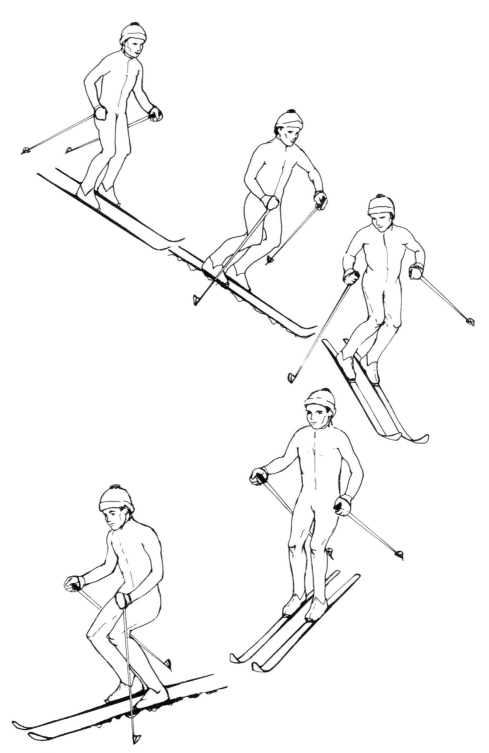

Fig 27   Parallel turns.

Fig 28   Telemark turn.

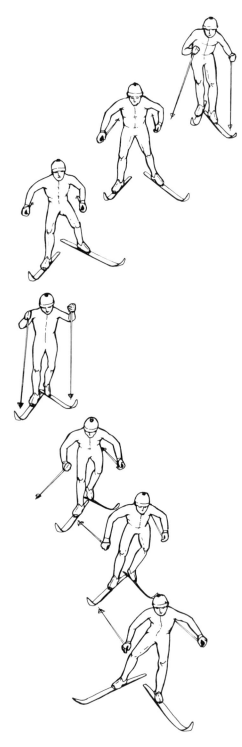

Fig 29   Double-sided skating.

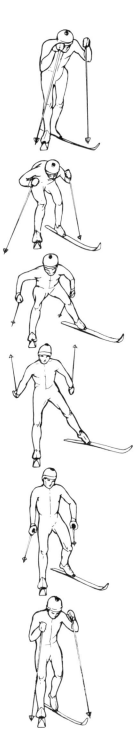

Fig 30   Single leg skating.

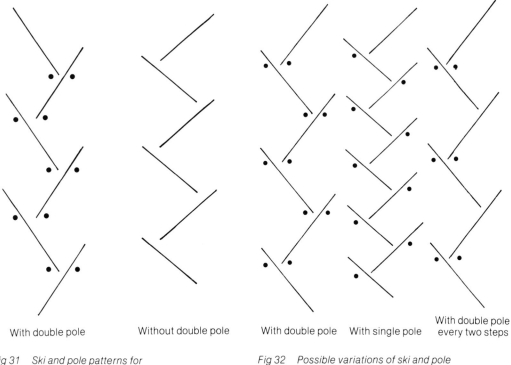

| With double pole | Without double pole | With double pole | With single pole | With double pole every two steps |

Fig 31   *Ski and pole patterns for double-sided skating.*

Fig 32   *Possible variations of ski and pole patterns for double-sided skating.*

weight is transferred to the opposite ski, which now enters the gliding phase. The gliding phase is on a flatter ski and may last for a considerable distance, depending on the angle of the slope or snow conditions.

On the flat, the poles can be used as for double poling between each skating step, or not at all. For climbing, the poles can be used between each skating step double or singly, or after every second skating step. The single-leg skate can also be useful when skiing in a prepared track.

4 Equipment

In Chapter 1 we briefly touched on the subject of equipment, pointing out the relative cheapness of cross-country skiing for the beginner, and its contrasting expense for the competitive or high-level skier who wants to take advantage of the latest developments in the equipment field.

BASIC CLOTHING

At whatever level you are skiing, the first essential is to dress correctly. Cross-country skiing is vigorous exercise, generating a considerable amount of body heat. The most common mistake amongst beginners is to overdress – you will often see skiers out on the trails wearing heavy anoraks and padded trousers, which not only inhibit freedom of movement, but also result in a free flow of perspiration. The removal of the heavy outer garments then leaves wet shirts and underclothes exposed to the cold air which chills or freezes them, leading at least to the risk of colds and at worst to the possibility of hypothermia.

The secret is to dress in layers which can be added to, or subtracted from, according to the air termperature and the amount of effort that you intend to put into your skiing. The layer nearest to the skin should, if possible, be made of polypropylene which has the property of allowing body moisture to pass through it and into outer layers, thus always keeping a dry garment next to the skin. To gain the full benefit of polypropylene, the vest should

be long-sleeved and pants should either be full-length 'long johns' or knee-length, if long socks are being worn. Some parts of a man's anatomy seem to feel the cold sooner than others, and plastic-fronted underpants are excellent at keeping the wind away from the more tender areas. There are several proprietary brands of polypropylene underwear on the market, of which the Norwegian Helly Hansen range is perhaps the best known in Britain.

Over the underwear, a long-sleeved shirt is advisable, with a polo neck to protect the exposed areas of the throat and neck from the cold. Commercially produced ski suits, which can be either one-piece or salopette and jacket, are the third essential layer. Both one-piece suits and salopettes offer the options of a full-length leg with a strap under the arch of the foot to ensure that the trouser leg does not ride up, or of a cut-off leg below the knee, necessitating a pair of long woollen stockings to complete the outfit. Until a few years ago this latter style was worn by everyone, but the full-legged suit has become increasingly popular. Few racers now wear anything else, although many tourers still prefer the warmth of long stockings, which can also be changed when wet without needing to change the whole suit. Cross-country suits come in a variety of thicknesses, with the body-hugging, stretch racing suits being the thinnest. Indeed, they are so lightweight that they are rarely worn without an over-suit, except in actual racing conditions.

With this exception, it is rarely necessary to wear anything over a ski suit, although

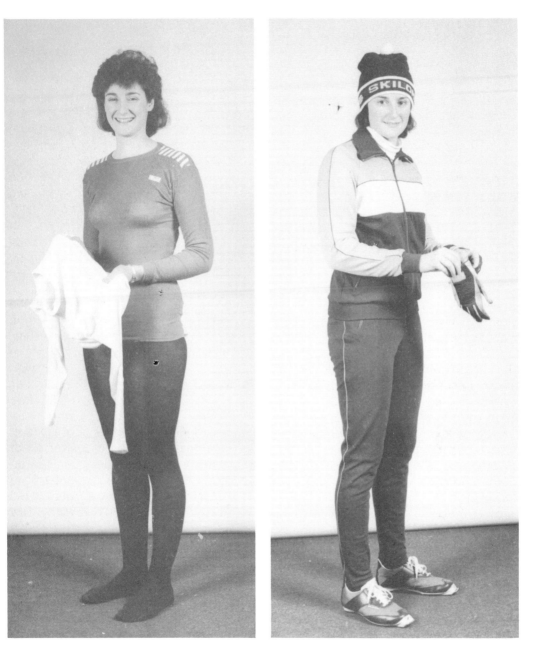

Fig 33   The first step in effective dressing
         for cross-country skiing is a neck to
         toe layer of polypropylene,
         followed by a polo neck long-
         sleeved shirt.

Fig 34   A one or two-piece suit, socks,
         shoes, hat and gloves complete
         the outfit.

tourers, particularly in mountain conditions, would be well advised to carry a cagoule with them in case they are caught out in the open in adverse weather conditions. Many people still choose to ignore commercially produced ski suits, and ski in a pair of old trousers or breeches and a warm sweater. Others cope perfectly well with a tracksuit. Two words of warning, though. First, make sure that the garments overlap well enough to cover the small of the back – a gap in the clothing here can lead to serious cold problems. Second, avoid wearing jeans or denim trousers. The material is unsuitable on a number of counts, lacking flexibility, retaining moisture and offering poor protection against the cold.

Fig 35   *The 75mm Nordic Norm is still the most popular general purpose boot/binding system on the market. It was once in almost universal use, but many manufacturers are now producing their own systems.*

FOOTWEAR (*Figs 35 to 39*)

The next problem is choosing the right pair of shoes or boots. Cross-country footwear comes in these two main forms, with the boot being used primarily for off-track touring, and the shoe for in-track recreational skiing and racing. The boot resembles a hill walking or hiking boot, whilst the shoe is very similar in shape to a pair of running spikes. Both have one thing in common – their means of attachment to the ski. The sole of the shoe or boot extends outwards beyond the toe. This protrusion fits into the binding and so attaches the skier to his ski by the toe only, leaving the heel free to rest on the ski, or to lift clear, as required.

The manufacturers of cross-country ski footwear have recently gone full circle. In the 1950s, in an effort to standardise boots and bindings, virtually all manufacturers adopted the Nordic Norm system, which consists of three holes in the underside of the extended toe of the boot, locating on to three upward facing pins on the binding, and being held firmly in place by the bale mechanism which clamped boot and ski together. For touring boots, the pins and matching holes covered a width of 75mm (3in), whilst racing shoes were narrower (to match the narrower racing skis) and were only 50mm (2in) apart. The only major firm not to conform to the 75mm (3in) and 50mm (2in) Nordic Norms was Adidas, who manufactured their own 38mm (1½in) shoe and binding.

For the consumer, this was an extremely acceptable situation. Buy any shoe (except Adidas) and it would fit any binding. Away from home, provided you had your own boots, you could borrow almost any pair of skis in the certain knowledge that boot and binding would be compatible. However, in the past decade, the situation has reversed. First, the French firm

Fig 36   *The Salomon Nordic system (SNS).*

Fig 37   *The Adidas 38mm.*

Equipment

Salomon invented the Salomon Nordic System (SNS), with an improved hinge arrangement at the toe, giving greater freedom to the foot and a longer stride. SNS swept the market, but it was a system that demanded not just the SNS shoe, but the compatible SNS binding as well. For a time all went well. Other shoe firms such as Alfa in Norway, Jalas in Finland and Hartjes in Austria started to make shoes under licence, using the SNS system. However, just short of a Salomon monopoly, the competitors started to wake up, to copy, and perhaps even to improve upon the SNS arrangement. By the 1986 season we were back where we started, with a plethora of bindings on the market, all made to fit individual makers' boots.

At the time of writing, the position is rather confused but there are certain glimmers of light among the chaos: for off-track touring, 75mm (3in) Nordic Norm still dominates the field, and you will not go far wrong in sticking with this tried and tested system. For in-track skiing and racing, the field of choice is much wider. Salomon, the new Nordic Norm system and Adidas are still the market leaders, but there are many other systems now available. The moral must be not to buy the first shoe you see, but to look around, try the system out if possible, and check before buying that replacement shoes and bindings will be readily available when they are needed.

Fig 38   The Trak Contact system.

Fig 39   To secure the boot to the ski, place the toe into the binding.
Ensure that the pins in the binding are fitted into the matching
holes in the underside of the toe of the boot.

Fig 40   Clamp down the bale mechanism to fix boot and binding in place.

ACCESSORIES

The apparently trivial items of ski clothing and equipment – socks, gloves, hats and backpacks – may not seem important, but they could be the small items that ruin the pleasure of a good day's skiing.

Socks and Gloves *(Fig 41)*

Socks or stockings may, as we have seen, be long or short, but they must be warm, they should always be kept clean to avoid blisters after a long day's ski, and the shoe must be large enough to accommodate them without cramping the toes and restricting movement and circulation.

Gloves come in various forms, depending on the type of skiing being undertaken. Racers wear very lightweight gloves, sufficient only to keep the fingers from going numb in the cold and to provide some protection against the chafing from the pole straps. They are comfortable and effective, but only for the purpose for which they were designed; something more

substantial will be needed for long-distance touring.

It is a matter of personal choice whether you opt for a substantial glove or for a mitt. The advantage of the former is that you will have greater control over your pole and can use your hand for other purposes without having to expose it to the cold, which might be the case if mitts are worn. Mitts, on the other hand, are warmer in very cold weather, are more likely to be waterproof (check for this when buying – even the best skiers fall over occasionally, and powder snow can make your hands very wet), and can be worn over a pair of inner, possibly thermal gloves. In very cold weather, and in exposed conditions, this combination of mitts and thermal inners is probably the most effective selection of all.

Hats *(Figs 42 & 43)*

A hat is always advisable. In very cold weather it can be pulled down over the ears, which are particularly susceptible to frost-bite, although the Norwegian firm

Equipment

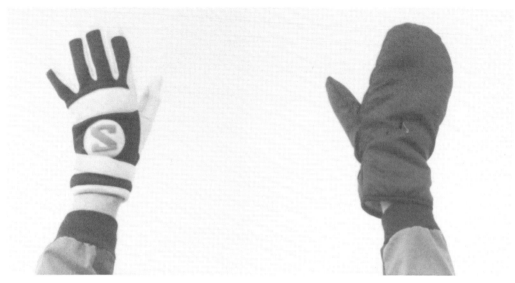

Fig 41 Gloves (left) are comfortable and offer greater control over your poling action, but mitts (right) afford greater protection against the cold.

Fig 43 A perspex visor is a useful piece of equipment when skiing in falling snow. This version, made by the Norwegian firm Swix, attaches to the sides of the ski hat with Velcro fasteners. Other makes use an adjustable band around the back of the head.

Fig 42 Ear-muffs are excellent at intermediate temperatures when a hat is not really necessary.

Swix do make very effective ear-muffs for this purpose. These look for all the world as if the skier is committing the heresy of bringing his personal stereo to disturb the peace of the loipe; it is only on close inspection that you realise there are no wires in sight. In really inclement weather, the benefits of a hat are obvious, keeping the head warm and dry against the elements. However, it is less generally recognised that the body's major heat loss is through the head, and that the wearing of a hat is therefore a very necessary and important precaution against hypothermia.

The type of hat to be worn is likely to vary according to the activity being undertaken. The racer will choose a very thin tuque, sufficient to keep in his body heat, but not so thick as to cause him to sweat unduly and face the irritation of perspiration running down his forehead and into his eyes. Tourers will almost certainly elect to wear a heavier garment and there are a number of balaclava-style hats available. In reasonable conditions these are worn like a normal ski hat, but can be unrolled if the weather worsens to cover the face and throat, with slits for the eyes and mouth, leaving the skier looking like nothing more than a bank robber. Some types have a built-in peak to keep snow and sun out of the eyes. Perspex peaks are also available, either with a strap around the back of the head, or attaching to the sides of the ski cap with Velcro fasteners.

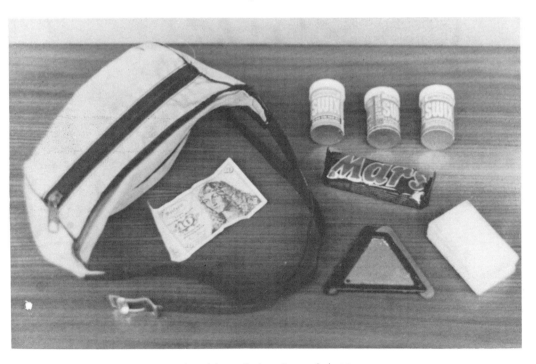

Fig 44   A bumbag and its contents – the minimum that can be carried on a day's recreational skiing when straying not too far from base. This includes three hard waxes, a cork, a scraper, local currency and some essential sustenance.

Packs *(Fig 44)*

For the bits and pieces that may be needed during a day's skiing, the choice lies between a backpack and a bumbag. Skiers operating in prepared tracks and not straying too far from base will generally take a bumbag, a small banana-shaped sac with a zip along the top, worn on the small of the back with a strap around the waist. An average bumbag will hold a few spare waxes and a cork, a couple of Mars bars and maybe a very lightweight cagoule – quite sufficient to meet the needs of the in-track recreational skier. A few notes of the local currency are another essential that should be carried in case of emergency, or perhaps to buy a drink at a cafe by the side of the loipe.

The tourer, who may be straying much further from the beaten track, must cater for a much wider range of possible problems. The extent of these, and therefore the amount of equipment he must carry to be prepared for them, will depend on the length of his tour and the terrain he will face. Touring is discussed at length in Chapter 6; a quick dip into those pages will make it obvious that a bumbag is never likely to satisfy the tourer's needs, and that his decision will be concerned with how large a backpack he needs to carry all his essential items.

SKIS *(Figs 45 & 46)*

The ski is far and away your most import-ant piece of equipment. However, choosing the right pair of skis is not as easy a matter as simply going into a shop and picking up the first pair that meets your eye. The make of ski is largely immaterial – models made by leading firms are more or

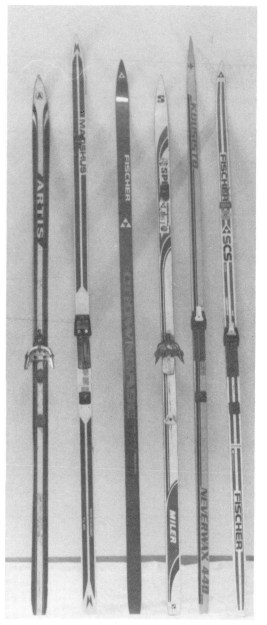

Fig 45 Six different types of cross-country ski. From the left, a wooden touring ski from Czechoslovakia, a light touring ski from Norway, a fish-scale base recreational ski from Austria, a racing trainer from Norway, a chemical-base (Neverwax) racing ski from Finland and a top racing ski from Austria.

less equal in the same price bands, and there is no one brand name that excels the others. Selecting a ski of the right length, the right flex and the right characteristics for in or off-track skiing does require a certain amount of knowledge, however, and it is well worth spending some time ensuring that you have made the correct choice, rather than buying in haste and repenting at your leisure.

Cross-country skis are made for a variety of different purposes. Until the mid-1970s, all skis were made of wood, but in the last decade fibreglass has become the universal material for ski construction, and it is now a matter for comment if a pair of old wooden skis are seen out on the tracks. Touring skis are broad, for stability, the widest being about 55mm (2¹⁄₅in), and may have metal edges to cope with ice and crust in untracked conditions. They may weigh as much as 2,500-3,000g (5lb 8oz–6lb 10oz) a pair. Recreational skis are thinner and lighter, while racing skis are fined down to 45mm (1⁴⁄₅in) in width and weights of less than 1,000 (2lb 3oz). Special skis are made for telemarking (sometimes known as cross-country downhill) and ski mountaineering. It is therefore essential to know your own needs and to buy skis that are suitable for the type of skiing to be undertaken. A pair of narrow, lightweight racing skis would sink right through the top surface if used in the untracked wilderness, whilst broad touring skis would prove an encumbrance to the racer, even in a long-distance citizens' marathon.

Your level of ability is also an important factor to take into account. Racing skis may look fast and flashy, but their parallel cut makes them difficult to handle and they are not recommended for the novice learning basic techniques. The 'waisted' construction (known as side-cut) of a touring ski, which is broader at the tip and tail than it is at the centre, makes it easier to control, particularly in the turns, and the

Fig 46 *The conventional way of choosing a ski of the right length for the user. Standing upright with the arm raised above the head, the tip of the ski should reach to just above the wrist.*

slower, more stable ski is more likely to result in quicker mastery of the initial steps.

Having decided on the type of ski to be bought, the next step is to find a pair of skis of the right length and camber. The traditional method for measuring skis is to stand upright with one arm held straight up above your head. With its tail on the floor beside you, the tip of the ski should reach to the palm of your hand (*see Fig 46*). This rule of thumb, by the way, applies to skis being used in the traditional methods. Racers wishing to buy skis for skating should select a pair at least 15cm (6in) shorter than the norm.

Getting the right length of ski is important – even 5cm (2in) of difference can dramatically alter skiing performance. In general terms, greater length gives greater speed, while less length gives greater control. If you are a beginner, you may want to buy a slightly shorter pair of skis than your height indicates, but only the very technically competent racer should look for greater length. One point to beware of if you are buying a new pair of skis of a different make to those used before: not all manufacturers use the same rule of measurement. Some measure the straight length of the ski, whilst others take their measurement along the curvature of the ski. One maker's 205cm (6ft 8½in) ski may therefore be the same as another's 210cm (6ft 10½in). Check before purchasing.

Testing the Camber
(*Figs 47 & 48*)

Before going any further, it is as well to check that the skis being bought are indeed a pair. All skis have an identification number which is normally stamped into the side wall of the ski. Check that the numbers match before carrying out the camber test. Cross-country skis do not lie flat on the ground. They are bowed in the middle, so that when they are unweighted, the tips and tails rest on the ground, while the centre portion (the camber pocket) is clear of the snow. This permits you to glide on tips and tails, then, when you wish to kick, your weight on the camber pocket will bring it in contact with the snow, enabling the wax to take effect. It is important that the camber should be both strong enough to hold you clear of the snow when the skis are unweighted, yet weak enough to make firm contact when your weight is put upon the single ski.

An experienced skier may judge the strength of the camber of a pair of skis by holding the pair of skis with the soles facing each other. Tips and tails will touch, whilst the arched camber pocket will remain apart. The strength of the camber can be judged by sqeezing the two skis together with your hand until the centre portions meet. The amount of force required to do this will be directly proportionate to the strength of the camber. This is not, however, a very accurate means of judgement, and a great deal of experience is necessary before skis can be assessed in this way.

The Paper Test

A much more objective judgement can be formed by using the 'paper test'. The skis must be placed side by side on a flat, hard floor (some ski shops have a specially designed board for this purpose, eliminating unevenness in the floor and the problems posed by soft carpets). Stand on the skis with your weight evenly balanced.

Fig 47   The paper test. With the weight evenly balanced on the skis, it
          should be possible to slide the paper under the camber pocket of
          the ski to a point approximately 30cm (12in) in front of the toe.

Fig 48   When the weight is shifted firmly on to the left ski, the paper
          should be trapped immovably under the foot. (Note how the
          camber on the unweighted ski in the lower photograph lifts the
          central portion of the ski clear of the ground.)

It should now be possible to slip a piece of paper under the camber pocket and to move it backwards and forwards from a point just behind the heel to about thirty centimetres (a foot) in front of the toes. If the paper will not move freely through this range, the camber of the skis is too soft for your weight and the skis should be rejected.

Assuming that the paper does move freely under the unweighted skis, the next part of the test is for you to put all your weight on one ski. The paper should now be trapped firmly between the ski and the floor. If it can still be moved, the skis' camber is too hard and will not provide the grip that is so essential in the kicking phase. Do not under any circumstances be persuaded into buying a pair of skis unless you have tried the paper test and you are satisfied with the results. If the camber is either too hard or too soft, that particular pair of skis is not for you – look again and test again until you find the pair that is just right.

Fish-scales

So far we have assumed that the skis being bought are waxable, and that their adhesion to the snow in the kicking phase is achieved by the application of a coat or coats of wax to the camber pocket of the ski. There are, however, numerous models of ski on the market that are designed to be used without wax. The earliest, and still the most commonplace of these, are 'fish-scales', so called because of the raised pattern in the shape of fish-scales on the underside of the camber pocket of the ski. The raised pattern is designed to permit the ski to slide forward across the snow, but to prevent it from sliding backwards. The benefits of fish-scales are that they eliminate the time consuming fuss of waxing and make light of uphill skiing in particular. Their disadvantage lies in the fact that the fish-scale acts as a partial brake on the flat and on downhill runs, reducing their overall effectiveness. They are a useful item to have in the store for use on those days when time is at a premium or when the temperature is hovering around zero and no wax will work, but under good conditions they are a poor substitute for waxable skis, and if you are a serious skier, you will have to look to wax if you want to make the most of your potential. The pros and cons are well summed up by two full-page adverts that appeared in an American magazine. The first, by a maker of fish-scale skis, carried the message: 'No wax; no hassle'. The following month a leading maker of waxes responded. Their advert carried the slogan: 'no wax; no glide'.

Besides fish-scales, a number of other no-wax systems, with a variety of names (for example, Multigrade, Neverwax, Microschuppen) are on the market, but none has yet been developed to the point where they make the waxable ski an endangered species.

Adapting to Conditions

Advanced skiers may wish to buy different skis to meet specific snow conditions. Icy or slushy snow, which will require the application of klister wax, demands a stiffer camber than powder snow, on which a hard wax will be used. An even softer camber may be used under very cold conditions, when the grip wax and the gliding wax being used may vary very little from one another. One firm, Karhu, has recognised this and sells its skis in a matching Matrix set. The day is fast approaching when the high-performance skier will carry his various skis about with him like a set of golf clubs; indeed, at top racing level this is already the case. For the beginner, however, one pair of skis will do to start with!

SKI POLES *(Figs 49 to 52)*

The one other essential piece of equipment is ski poles. Previously made of bamboo, they are now more usually to be found in aluminium, fibreglass or carbon fibre. Like skis, they vary according to the purpose for which they are to be used. The pole itself

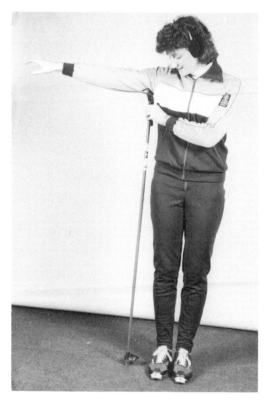

Fig 50   The pole should reach from the floor to the armpit of the skier.

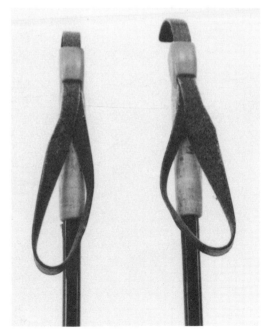

Fig 49   Poles come in pairs, right and left-handed. With the pole straps hanging down and facing the skier, the lower strap is always on the side of the thumb as the hand is inserted into the loop.

will vary in weight (and expense) from the sturdy, cylindrical tourer's pole, to the extremely lightweight, extremely expensive, carbon fibre or boron racing pole. Baskets too will range from the traditional round basket, now only used in deep, soft snow, to the small plastic racing basket designed to give maximum thrust and minimum drag on hard-packed racing or recreational tracks. The length of a ski pole is normally measured from the floor to the armpit of the skier. Racers and fast recreational skiers may elect to use poles up to 5cm (2in) longer than this, and skaters will need at least 10cm (4in) more again.

Fig 51   Baskets on poles are designed for specific uses. From the left: an old-fashioned but still effective touring basket; a recreational basket; two racing baskets for in-track use.

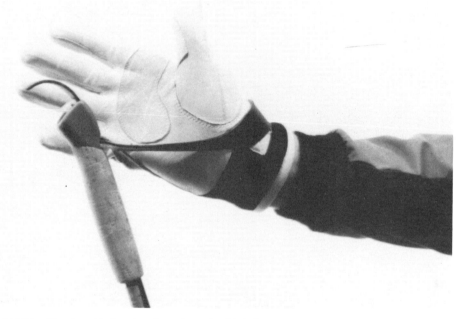

Fig 52   The hand must be placed in the strap from the underside before grasping the pole. A common fault amongst beginners is to attempt to put the hand through the loop of the strap from above. This results in the strap being a hindrance rather than a help and prevents efficient use of the pole.

CONCLUSIONS

The selection of the right equipment is the key to the enjoyment of cross-country skiing. Analyse the sort of skiing that you want to do, then buy equipment designed for that purpose. Take advice, look around and do not buy until you are certain that you have found what you want. Do not allow yourself to be pressured into a hasty purchase by smooth sales patter. If you buy from the specialist shops you are unlikely to receive bad advice, but if you do not see what you want, wait until you find it. You will have all winter to regret the purchase made in haste against your better judgement, and all winter to enjoy the right equipment, bought with forethought for the right conditions.

5 Ski Preparation and Maintenance

In Chapter 4 we discussed briefly the pros and cons of waxless and waxable skis. Although this chapter is based largely on the assumption that you are using waxable skis, much of it is equally applicable to waxless skis and their protection in order to gain the maximum benefit from them. It is often forgotten that the expressions 'waxless' and 'no-wax' refer only to the camber pocket of the ski. The tips and tails of the skis still require regular attention to preserve them from the ravages of daily use and to improve their gliding capability. Those parts of this chapter that deal with the preparation of new skis and the treatment of glide zones therefore apply equally to both waxable and waxless skis.

WAXING (*Fig 53*)

Why do we need to wax at all? The answer lies in the crystalline texture of the snow. Fresh snow crystals are large and pointed, and will remain so for some time under cold conditions. As they become older or warmer, the crystals become smaller, rounder and less sharply pointed. Just as the snow crystals change, so the moisture content and temperature of the snow is subject to change; the snow base on which you are skiing is an infinitely variable surface.

The object of waxing is to ensure that the ski has the best possible adhesion to the snow during the kick phase and the best possible glide, whatever the conditions. This is achieved by selecting the appropriate waxes to meet the temperature, humidity and snow conditions of the day. Hard waxes give the best grip when the snow is cold and fresh, while klisters fulfil the same function when conditions are wet or icy. If too hard a wax is chosen, the snow crystals will be unable to penetrate it, there will be a loss of grip and the ski will slide backwards when pressure is applied to it during the kick phase; if too soft a wax is used, the crystals will penetrate too far into the wax and will cling to it, slowing the skier down and, in the worst cases, causing the snow to ball up under the ski.

A well-waxed ski is not only faster, carrying the skier further for the expenditure of the same amount of effort, but it is more easily controlled since its empathy with the snow surface enables it to be turned more easily, either on the flat or in downhill situations.

Hard Waxes (*Figs 55 & 56*)

It is normal in any discussion on waxing to start with the range of hard waxes. These are normally sold in tubs, and are colour-coded for use at differing temperatures. One word of caution is necessary here: some manufacturers base their recommended range of use on snow temperatures, whilst others, notably the Norwegian firm Swix, base their recommended range on air temperatures. It is therefore sensible to start by using the products from one particular wax company and to stick to them until you have gained sufficient

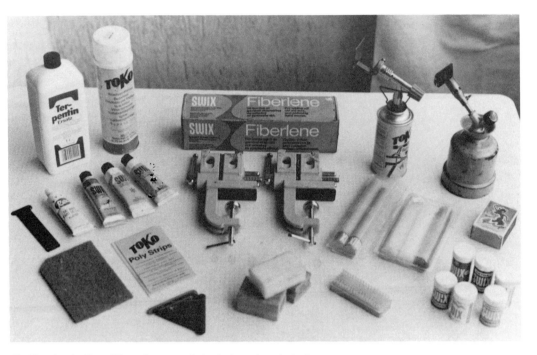

Fig 53   A selection of items from a well-stocked wax box, including:
(rear), white spirit and commercial wax remover, Fiberlene (a
lint-free material for ski cleaning), two waxing torches; (centre),
four tubes of klister with spreader, a pair of ski clamps, two
packets of glide wax and a box of matches; (front), Fibretex and
poly strips for repair work, a scraper, three corks, a brush and a
range of hard waxes.

experience to experiment with other companies' products.

Which producer should one choose? Any reputable firm is acceptable, but it is worth considering that any firm's products are designed in the main for home consumption and are manufactured with local snow conditions in mind. You are therefore unlikely to go too far wrong in trying the 'home brand', Swix in Norway, Rex in Finland, Ex-Elite in Sweden, Toko in Switzerland, or Rode in Italy, for example. However, this merely makes the starting choice easier, it does not imply that any of the waxes will not work equally well; all those mentioned are highly reputable firms

whose products perform perfectly satisfactorily all over the world in a variety of differing snow conditions.

Hard waxes are the easiest of all to apply. Simply take off the top of the tub, peel back a little of the protective covering and crayon gently on to the ski from a point roughly beneath the heel plate to about thirty centimetres (a foot) in front of the toe. Although this is the ideal waxing zone, beginners will gain greater adhesion by extending this area both backwards and particularly forwards, perhaps by as much as thirty centimetres (a foot), and then gradually reducing the waxed zone as experience and competence increase.

Ski Preparation and Maintenance

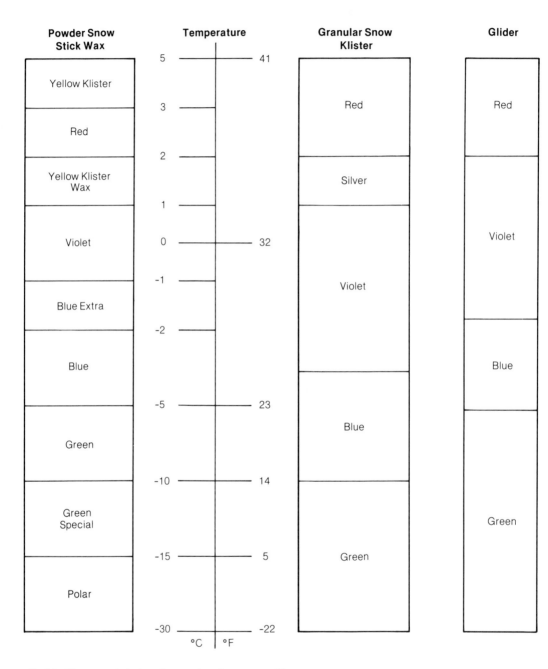

Fig 54   The correct choice of waxes to suit snow conditions and temperatures.

Fig 55   Stick wax must be crayoned on to
the base of the ski . . .

Fig 56   . . . and then rubbed smooth with
a cork.

Most modern skis are produced with markings on the sole to help in judging the right area to be waxed. When the wax has been crayoned on, take a cork (generally synthetic nowadays), and rub the wax firmly but lightly until it is visible only as a light film covering the surface of the kicking zone of the ski. The objective is to smooth out the wax, paying particular attention to any lumps or blobs that may have formed in rubbing it on. However, the friction and heat of the rubbing should smooth out the wax, it is not an exercise in brute strength. Some authorities advocate rubbing from the point of the ski towards the tail, but it is doubtful if there is any real merit in this and there will certainly be no advantage to the touring skier.

When the ski has been waxed, try it out. If it slips backwards, apply a second coat of the same wax; if it still slips, extend the length of the wax along the ski, particularly in front of the boot. If this does not do the trick, apply another layer of a warmer wax. Note a *warmer* wax: it is a general rule that warm waxes can be applied on top of colder waxes, but not vice versa. If in doubt as to the correct wax to choose, always start with the colder wax to which a warmer wax can be applied if necessary. If you start with a warmer wax and get it wrong, you are faced with the aggravating chore of scraping it all off the ski and starting again.

To increase the durability of your wax for long tours or races, a base wax can be used to bind the hard wax to the ski, or alternatively one layer of a colder wax can be used as a binder. The base wax or binder should be warmed well into the ski by passing a torch or iron gently over it. It must then be allowed to cool before being corked lightly to ensure smoothness before the grip wax of the day is applied as normal.

Hard waxes are for fresh snow. In Scandinavia and North America, where cold temperatures and regular snowfalls are the norm, it may be possible to go through a whole season without using any other form of grip wax. However, nature does not always make life so easy. Whenever snow has been transformed from its original state, hard waxes will not work effectively and klister waxes must be used.

Klister Waxes (*Fig 57*)

The transformation of the snow from its original state - that is to say, the breaking down of the sharp points of the snow crystal until the crystal becomes rounded and granular - will occur if the snow is subjected to temperatures above freezing point. It will then melt and may become wet, mushy or even sodden with rain. While this situation persists, klister waxes are needed. Frequently, after a warm afternoon of spring sunshine, the top surface of the snow will melt, only for the temperature to drop again at night, freezing the upper layers of snow and creating an icy crust on top of the underlying powder. Heavy use of the loipe during the day can also melt the snow within the tracks, which will then be left, after a cold night, glazed and icy in the morning, although the surrounding snow may still retain its powdery appearance. In these conditions klister wax will either be used on its own or, if the ice is not too severe and is mixed with powder snow, klister may be used as a base wax, or skare, with a hard wax applied on top.

Fig 57 *Klister may be applied to the ski in a straight line on either side of the central tracking groove. Applying it in a herringbone fashion, as shown in this photograph, helps to ensure that the klister is spread thinly and evenly over the desired length of the camber pocket.*

Klister waxes come in tubes like toothpaste. They are sticky waxes which must be applied with great care if they are not to spread all over the sides and top surface of the ski, as well as on to your hands and clothing. Being very sticky, they give effective grip but can also act as a brake during the gliding phase; they are therefore generally applied over a slightly shorter area of the ski than are hard waxes, and many skiers keep a pair of skis with a particularly stiff camber for use in klister conditions. The stiffer ski will hold the klister clear of the snow until the pressure of the kick is applied to the waxed area. The warmer klisters (red, yellow and silver) can usually be applied satisfactorily outdoors and rubbed in with the hand. The colder klisters are much harder and must be applied to the ski indoors, where the tube can be warmed to soften the klister before spreading.

The technique is to squeeze out the klister in very thin strips on each side of the tracking groove. Pass the flame from a waxing torch very carefully up and down over the klister until it starts to run and can be smoothed out carefully with a spreader to form an even tacky layer on either side of the base of the ski. While warming the klister, keep the torch at a good distance from the ski and do not allow the flame to play on any particular point of the ski for more than a fraction of a second. Intense, direct heat will bubble the base of the ski, ruining it in an instant. When the klister has been spread, put it outside to cool before smoothing it out with a synthetic waxing cork. Remember that klister must always be applied thinly; the most common error in applying klister is to spread it too thickly. As with stick waxes, a fine layer of a colder klister can be warmed into the ski as a base for a warmer klister. This base klister must be so fine that it is hardly detectable once smoothed into the ski.

There is no doubt that it pays to spend the time and effort to learn how to wax properly. Performance will be immeasurably improved on a properly waxed ski. For those who do not want the hassle of choosing and testing to find the right wax, or who may anticipate skiing through a range of conditions during the day, 'universal' hard waxes and klisters are available, with each wax covering a wide temperature range. 'Wet' and 'Dry' touring waxes fulfil the same function. They are an effective compromise, but like all compromises they are less effective than finding the right solution to the problem posed by the conditions of the day.

Waxing for Racing

Racers, particularly those taking part in the long distance citizens competitions, may be faced with particular waxing problems, as the temperature and snow conditions may change several times during an event lasting up to nine or ten hours. Eventually the only solution may be to stop and rewax, but much valuable time can be saved by thinking ahead and, if necessary, breaking the normal waxing rules. Let us suppose that the race starts at 8 a.m., with a temperature of –10 degrees centigrade, but that as the day progresses and the sun grows warmer, temperatures 5 degrees higher may be anticipated. It may be necessary to wax with blue hard wax (for later in the day) but to cover it with a layer of green wax to cope with the early morning cold. We have already seen that cold wax will not stick on top of a warmer wax; the green will therefore wear off in the early kilometres, leaving a correctly waxed ski as the day warms up. There is a secret to this: be sure that when the warm wax has been applied, the ski is put outside and left to become very cold. The colder wax may then be crayoned on gently.

If this approach is not possible, a mixture of waxes may be the only answer. The recommended 'wax of the day' for the 1983 Engadin Ski Marathon, in which wide temperature variations were expected, was a mixture of blue, violet and red klisters, with a layer of blue special hard wax on top. It worked!

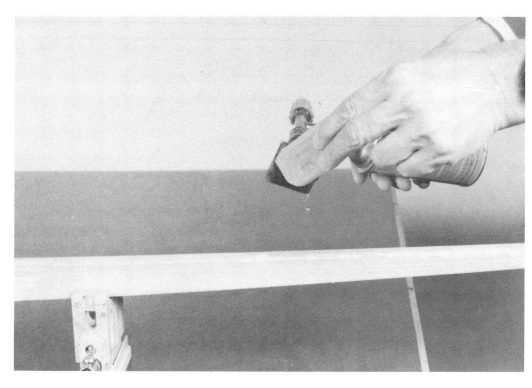

Fig 58   Waxing glide zones. The wax is allowed to drip on to the base of
the ski.

Waxing New Skis
(*Figs 58 to 60*)

Whilst the correct grip wax must be applied before each outing - unless there is still plenty left on from the previous day, and conditions have not changed - the waxing of glide zones, for all but the racer, is less critical. Glide zone treatment begins with the purchase of a new pair of skis. These must be thoroughly cleaned to remove dirt that they may have picked up in storage or transit. When the skis are clean, they must be thoroughly sanded to remove any irregularities still remaining in the base after factory treatment. Fit the ski into a stable waxing bench or vice, taking care to pad the metal so as not to damage the side

walls of the skis, and working from tip to tail with a sanding block, rub down the ski for five to ten minutes with coarse grade 100 silicon carbide paper, then sand again with grade 150 paper, and finish the job with grade 180. Be careful not to neglect the centre groove. After sanding, clean down the skis with water or a proprietary wax remover. The skis are then ready to be waxed.

For the first waxing, use violet or universal glide wax, holding the wax against a waxing iron (an ordinary electric iron set at 'wool' temperature will do equally well) and allowing it to drip along the whole length of the ski. Smooth it in by running the iron over the waxed sections and then leave the ski outside to cool. After about thirty

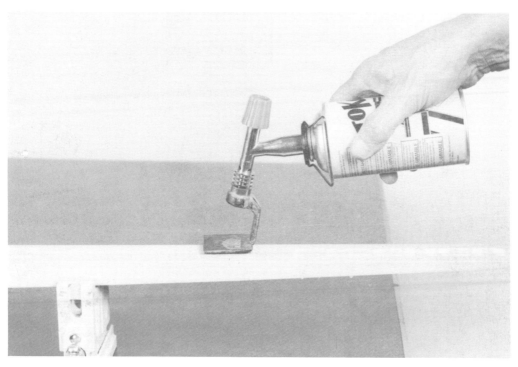

Fig 59   The wax is then smoothed in with a hot iron.

minutes scrape the wax off with a plastic scraper, working from tip to tail until there is no more wax left to remove. Using a rounded edge, as found on the spreaders supplied with klisters, clean out all the wax which has entered the central tracking groove, and also scrape the sides of the skis to remove the little rivulets of wax which may have run over the edges. Some ski manufacturers recommend treating the tip and tail glide zones only and leaving the camber pocket, which will receive grip wax, free. If the whole length of the ski is treated, particular care must be taken, using a *metal* scraper, to remove all residual wax from the camber pocket. Be careful at this stage to avoid damaging the glide zones of the skis; never use a metal scraper on the glide zones.

When the scraping has been finished, the result should be a smooth base from which all glide wax has been removed. Only the wax which has penetrated into the base of the ski remains. To complete the process, stroke a nail brush over the glide zones from tip to tail four or five times to break up the surface and prevent suction when the skis are in contact with the snow. The glide zones of the skis are now ready for use and the camber pocket is ready to receive grip wax.

The sanding process need only be repeated occasionally during the season when the skis have become excessively dirty; waxing of the glide zones must be done more frequently, perhaps once a week if the skis are being used daily in prepared tracks. The procedure is exactly

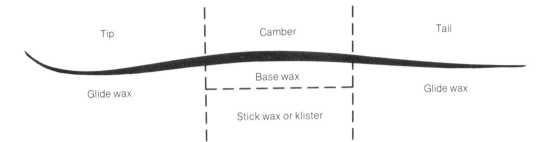

Fig 60   Profile of a cross-country ski. The tip and tail must be glide waxed, whilst the arched camber section, which rides clear of the snow during the glide phase, receives the grip wax which can be penetrated by the snow crystals, giving adhesion during the kick phase.

as outlined above, but choosing the glide wax appropriate to the prevailing temperature and conditions. On these occasions, make sure that the glide wax is not allowed to drip on to the central camber section, which must be left clear to take the grip wax. Any glide wax which does intrude on to this central section must be removed with a metal scraper.

Removing Wax *(Fig 61)*

Waxes, particularly grip waxes and especially klisters, will usually need to be removed before a new wax can be applied. The first step is to take off as much wax as possible using a scraper, then take a torch and, running it lightly backwards and forwards over the waxed area, remove the melted wax with a piece of rag. Take care when doing this not to damage the base of the ski with the flame, and also be careful not to set fire to the rag, which will become highly flammable once impregnated with wax and wax remover. Finally, clean off the ski with white spirit or a proprietary wax remover. If using white spirit, wash down and dry the ski before applying new wax.

Fig 61   Scraping the residual wax off a ski using a plastic scraper.

REPAIRS

Where bases are damaged, simple repairs can be effected by lighting a P-tex candle (available from all good ski shops) and dripping it carefully on to the hole or groove in the base of the ski. Leave it to dry, then level it off with a fine file or scraper before sanding it down with coarse and fine paper. With practice, a very professional repair can be achieved on even the most alarming looking holes and gashes.

PREPARING WAXLESS SKIS

The glide zones of waxless skis need to be prepared in exactly the same way as those of waxable skis, but it is often overlooked that the no-wax kicker zones (camber pockets) also require periodic attention. Before each outing they should be sprayed with silicone – available in commercially produced canisters – which not only prevents soft snow from balling-up under the ski, but also inhibits oxidation and is an essential part of ski maintenance.

PREPARING WOODEN SKIS

A final word on the preparation of wooden skis will not be out of place, before they disappear for ever from our ken. Wood needs totally different treatment from fibreglass. It will, in fact, glide quite well with no preparation at all, but proper treatment will protect it against the damp which otherwise soon penetrates the wood and causes deterioration of the ski.

The first step is to apply a solution of pine tar to the entire base and heat it in well with a waxing torch, passing the flame backwards and forwards over it until it begins to bubble very gently. An iron is not very practical for this purpose – especially if you want to press your trousers with it at a later date! The excess pine tar which is not soaked up by the ski must be wiped off with a cloth leaving the base of the ski dry to the touch, but with the rich dark colour and pervading odour of pine tar.

When the skis have cooled, hard waxes can be applied. Glide waxes are not necessary and the appropriate hard wax can be applied over the whole length of the ski. Wood skis too can take klister, but in these conditions the klister must be applied in the same manner as for synthetic skis and kept as short as possible underfoot if forward progress is not to come to a sudden halt.

The preparation and waxing of skis is not, as some would suggest, an arcane art. To be practised successfully, it requires knowledge and experience – knowledge not just of skis and waxes, but of the ever-changing snow conditions which you may have to face. To some it may seem to be an unnecessary chore, but it is one which, once accepted, will improve your performance, increase your knowledge and, undoubtedly, enhance your enjoyment of cross-country skiing, as you slowly achieve mastery over the continual challenges posed by temperature, weather and varying snow conditions.

6 Ski Touring

INTRODUCTION

Ski touring – the challenge of the high mountains and the solitude of the open spaces – is for many people what cross-country skiing is all about.

Each of the Scandinavian countries has its own organisation devoted exclusively to touring skiing. The DNT (Norwegian Tourist Association) maintains a network of well kept overnight huts in Norway, in such areas as the Hardanger Vidda and the Jotunheim, while their Finnish equivalent, the Suomen Lattu, run regular hut to hut and snow holing courses in the remoter parts of the country, notably in the huge and unspoilt Lapland National Park.

Further south, in the Alpine areas, ski touring is perhaps slightly more commercialised and it need not be an altogether uncomfortable experience to complete the 100km (62 miles) Black Forest trail or the Grande Traversée du Jura, the famous GTJ. On both of these trails you can ski from one hotel or gite to the next and the track between resting places is well manicured. The Traversée du Vercors, in France, is in rather wilder country with only the occasional log cabin for overnight accommodation. These are not kept stocked and travellers must carry everything they need on their back. The Traversée crosses a wilderness park and individuals are not allowed to undertake it on their own. Beautiful as it is, it can be easily completed in two days and will not pose a challenge to the hardy adventurer.

In Britain, the nature of the climate and geography means that ski touring in mountainous areas such as the Pennines, the Lake District or the Cairngorms provides the most regular opportunity for avid skiers to get out on snow. It is on this aspect of ski touring that we have concentrated our attention in this chapter.

MOUNTAIN TOURING IN GREAT BRITAIN

It has been said that once you have mastered the basics of Nordic skiing, it is possible to get into trouble in the mountains of Great Britain much faster, simply because increased speeds and less effort are involved. However, you could argue that a skilled skier gets off the mountains much quicker should he have to, in, for example, deteriorating weather.

The British climate dictates that most skiing will be done in the high mountain areas of Great Britain, and therefore you should pay close attention to the British Mountaineering Council's Mountain Safety Code.

Safety Precautions

Before You Set Out

1. Carry a map at least 1:63,360 (1in) or 1:50,000 in scale.
2. Have with you spare warm clothing, especially gloves, balaclava and extra sweater, as well as windproof and waterproof outer garments.

3. Carry emergency rations (and don't eat them *en route*!).

4. Carry a whistle, torch and small first-aid kit in case of accident.

5. Leave information of your route and keep to it, for example, at your youth hostel, hotel, guest house, or at a police station, information centre or mountain rescue post, or best, on day trips, at home.

6. Until you have a great deal of experience, never go out on mountains alone – the safest number is four or more.

7. Know where the local mountain rescue posts and nearest telephones are situated.

Planning Your Route

1. Estimate the time that it will take, and make sure that you have sufficient hours of daylight, leaving a wide safety margin for any miscalculation or delay.

2. Remember that the weather can change very quickly. If conditions are bad in the valley, they will be considerably worse higher up, and a walk that you found easy in the summer may be very different in winter. Always plan your route in relation to the prevailing conditions and be very cautious about what you attempt in bad weather.

3. Do not overestimate your own stamina or ability.

4. Treat the hills with very great respect in snow conditions, and do not go up snow-covered mountains unless you are familiar with the use of an ice axe. Plan your day accordingly.

Out on the Hills

1. Never let anyone get left behind – a party should always stay together, moving at the pace of the slowest.

2. Never be afraid of turning back if weather conditions worsen or you realise that the route is too long or too hard for you.

3. If you wear boots soled with composition rubber, be sure that you are aware of their limitations – they are slippery on wet grass, lichened, mossy or greasy rock, ice and hard snow.

4. On a steep slope be very careful not to dislodge loose rocks on to those below. When rock scrambling, a party should keep close together so that if a stone is dislodged it will not have had much time to gather momentum should it hit one of the party below. On a scree slope it is best to zigzag or adopt an arrowhead formation.

On the Descent

The majority of mountaineering accidents occur on the descent from a peak when, once the climb is over, there is a tendency to become hasty and careless. Particular points to note are:

1. Don't take a short cut – the path invariably takes the safest, easiest and quickest way.

2. Always descend the longer, more gradual side of a mountain. Scrambling down steep, rocky ground can be very dangerous.

3. Never run, slide or glissade down a slope unless you can see a clear way to the bottom.

4. Do not follow streams downhill. They may end in a waterfall.

Losing Your Way

If you get lost, stay together, sit down, and keep calm. Carefully work out from the map your approximate position and consider whether to stop or continue. If the latter, decide in which direction you ought to go, and then trust your compass. If a member of the group is exhausted or if you find that darkness is descending and you are still on the mountain, it is better not to try and get down in the dark unless the whole group can move on and you are on a path or quite certain of the route. Map reading at night is extremely difficult, and you cannot tell the difference between a boulder and a precipice. Accept the fact that you are out for the night, look around for some shelter from the wind, and make yourself as comfortable as possible. You should, of course, be carrying spare clothing and emergency rations.

If the weather and the visibility are good, you will be able to descend next morning to another valley. Then get word to your original destination before a search party is sent out. If at dawn the weather and visibility are poor, so that you feel it is still too dangerous to attempt to move, give the international distress signal (six blasts of a whistle at ten-second intervals; reply, three blasts at twenty-second intervals), in case a rescue party is searching for you.

Emergency Bivouacs

1. Choose a sheltered spot out of the wind or, if necessary, build a wind-break out of rocks.
2. Put on your spare clothing, with dry clothes next to your skin. Use your rucksack or rope to sit on. A groundsheet, plastic mac, or a thick bag of industrial polythene of not less than gauge 500 will protect you against the wind and rain and it it is a good idea always to carry one of these in your rucksack. Bags of this thickness are used regularly in high mountain bivouacs and could in an emergency, save

your life in Britain. Do *not* use the thin polythene bags that can be bought in most stores for covering or storing blankets.
3. If it is very cold, try to stay awake and keep warm by frequently exercising your arms and legs. Make sure that none of your clothing is restricting circulation, particularly at extremities. Slacken your boot laces.

Bivouacs on Snow

Snow shelters can provide protection against the weather and much information is now available on their construction. The making of snow shelters can be time consuming and if possible you should allow for this.

1. Dig or cut a cave into a slope, keeping the entrance small and hollowing the cave out inside with an arched roof. A shelter of this kind will give complete protection from the wind and, once inside, your bodily warmth will soon raise the temperature above freezing point.
2. If on level snow, excavate a hole 60cm (2ft) deep and then use your ice axe to scrape the snow into a compact wall or walls for a wind break. Ice axes and ground sheets can then be used to form a cover or lean-to shelter.

Summary

Most accidents in mountains are due to one or more of the following reasons:

1. Carelessness.
2. Overestimation of your physical stamina or technical ability.
3. Lack of observation.
4. Lack of knowledge.
5. Failure to act together as a group.

You alone can guard against the first two dangers or causes of accidents. When you go out skiing, always go prepared for the unexpected – a sudden change in the weather, a delay or a set-back which leads to an unforeseen night out in the open. Remember that if you are wholly unprepared, a night out in winter conditions can be fatal.

Weather

The greatest hazard in winter is almost certainly the British climate. The typical winter weather patterns in Britain are as severe as anywhere in the world and a detailed check of a good and updated weather forecast before a mountain tour is essential.

The BBC news and press weather forecasts are very general and do not give enough detailed information for hill walkers, mountaineers or skiers. These forecasts given are for sea level and need to be converted for the hills and mountains. As a general rule, wind speeds can be multiplied by two and a half to give the speed at the top of a 1,000m (3,280ft) mountain, and temperature decreases by 2-3 degrees Centigrade for every 305m (1,000ft) climbed. This is known as the lapse rate.

In 1985 the Meteorological Office and British Telecom successfully introduced a Mountain Line weather forecasting service for the mountain areas of Scotland. The forecasts are updated twice a day at 0600 hours and 1700 hours.

MOUNTAIN SKIING

It is essential for mountain skiers to be able to recognise and cope with icy conditions.

They should realise the limitations of Nordic skiing equipment in such conditions. If the edges of your skis are razor sharp and you are using a good mountain boot and binding system, life will certainly be a lot easier for you, and you will be able to cope with most snow conditions.

Safety

When assessing a slope before attempting to ski down it or across it, always take into account the consequences of a fall and slide. What is the run out like – long, steep or rocky? Can you see all the way to the bottom? If you do fall on steep, hard-packed snow or ice and you happen to be wearing smooth nylon or Gortex outer clothing, the speed at which you accelerate down the fall line can make a Porsche look docile. When you are uncertain of your ability to cope with the angle of the slope or the snow conditions, and the consequences of a fall are serious, take your skis off, put your crampons on, take hold of your ice-axe and *walk* down.

Arresting a Slide
with Ski Sticks (Fig 62)

When skiing on a fairly steep slope where a fall is likely, it is a good idea to take your hands out of your ski straps and prepare to use the ski stick tips as a brake. Once you have fallen, take hold of one or both ski sticks just above the basket, hold the ski sticks in line with your chest so that the weight of your upper body can be applied to the sticks and the bottom five or so centimetres (two inches) of the sticks can be forced into the snow. Whilst this technique may not bring you to a complete stop, it will reduce the speed of the slide.

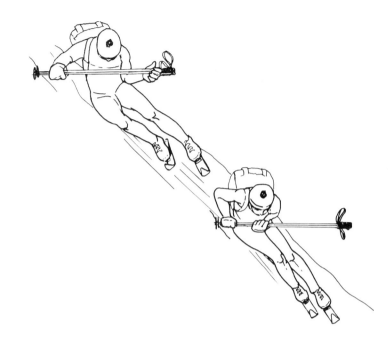

Fig 62   *Self-arrest using ski sticks.*

Turning your Skis on Ice

It is generally best to use the stem or parallel turn when skiing on ice. Remember to keep as much of your body weight as possible on the turning or lower ski. A good edge set and angulation (keep the knees into the hill) will ensure that the edges have a good chance of holding. The telemark turn is of little use in icy conditions as it is slow in comparison with other turns through the fall line, and it is much more difficult to hold an edge because it is a banked turn.

Using Ski Sticks for Support (Fig 63)

On a downhill run, the ski sticks can be used to control speed and increase stability. The techniques illustrated are particularly useful when skiing over sastrugi or snow of constantly changing consistencies.

Telescopic Nordic Ski Sticks

A number of manufacturers are now producing telescopic Nordic ski sticks. Being able to shorten your poles for the downhill runs is useful, while on a long ascending traverse it is much more comfortable to be able to shorten the uphill ski pole.

Skins

Adhesive skins will enable you to climb quickly with much less effort, but they cannot be used in conjunction with wax so you must choose one or the other unless you are prepared to clean off your skis before applying skin. The classic tour of the

Fig 63   *Use of ski sticks for support.*

Four Tops of the Cairngorms in Scotland is a good example of a tour more suited to using skins, since there are two main very steep ascents and the rest is undulating terrain or downhill.

Remember that the ski soles must be completely dry and free of wax before applying the skins.

NAVIGATION

Even on those rare winter days when the sun shines, the sky is cloudless and there is a couple of centimetres (an inch) or so of soft powder snow lying on top of a firm base, navigation is much more difficult than on a pleasant summer's day. The reason is that paths and streams are often totally covered and features are distorted by drifted snow. There simply is not the same amount of visible information to be related to the map. If you are in thick cloud on a snow covered terrain, you will really find navigation very difficult. Instinct or a sense of direction will not help you at all. To be able to navigate accurately in 'white-out' conditions (where the sky and ground blend into one) requires considerable skill and practice. Only the compass and pacing your progress are going to prevent you from becoming totally disorientated.

When caught out in such conditions the best thing to do is to take a safe bearing from the map, take your skis off and start walking. It is almost impossible to follow a compass bearing accurately in white out conditions on skis, and it is quite impossible to judge the distance you are covering unless you are on foot and counting paces - the average is about 60 double paces per 100m (328ft) normally, but deep snow or a head wind will increase the paces to about 80 double paces per

100m (328ft).

One of the best ways of practising and improving navigation is to try your hand at orienteering. Thrashing through thick woods also requires skilled compass work and accurate pacing or timing and the consequences of getting it wrong are not too serious. Unless you are skilled in the use of map and compass, you should not be touring the hills and mountains of Great Britain in winter.

AVALANCHES

The study of snow and avalanches is a complex and inexact science. Any Nordic skier who has mastered the art of waxing his skis in Britain will know of the many different snow types and will probably have developed a curiosity or interest in snow structures. He will therefore find the study of avalanche conditions interesting.

It is our intention to cover only general rules and guidelines in this section and we would strongly recommend that Nordic skiers intending to travel in Great Britain make a separate and detailed study (*see* Further Reading).

To begin with, it would be wrong to believe that avalanches occur solely in mountainous areas. Indeed, Britain's worst avalanche incident took place in Lewes, Sussex, in 1836, destroying several cottages and killing eight inhabitants. Almost any snow-covered slope can avalanche, and when ski touring you should be constantly assessing likely risks and identifying areas to avoid.

Even before setting out on a ski tour, a study of weather patterns will help to give an indication of the snow conditions you are likely to encounter during your tour. Any tour undertaken within twenty-four

hours of a heavy snowfall is likely to be on unstable snow. Strong winds will be constantly moving snow around the hills and forming large and unstable deposits on leeward slopes. However, snow conditions can change in a matter of hours and the only way to test the stability of a slope is to dig a snow pit at the foot and to one side of the slope you intend to cross. The pit should be dug down to ground level and then a careful examination of the snow profile should take place. Any weak layers or marked changes can then be identified.

A further test of inserting a shovel or ice-axe about thirty centimetres (twelve inches) behind the wall of your pit and then levering towards it will give an indication of weak layers within the profile. If there is any doubt in your mind, don't cross the slope.

It is important to remember that information gained by digging a snow pit is only good for that one particular slope. It will serve only as a rough indication for other slopes of the same aspect, but will have absolutely no bearing on nearby slopes of a different aspect.

General Rules

The following points should be observed when crossing dangerous slopes:

1.   Don't.
2.   If there is no alternative, cross one at a time whilst the rest of the group watch from a safe position.
3.   Trail a rope or cord.
4.   Carry an avalanche transceiver.
5.   Go straight down the fall line if possible.
6.   Loosen rucksacks, safety straps, etc.
7.   Cross high.
8.   Avoid convexities.

If you are caught in an avalanche, remember the following points:

1. Call out, and try to jump or ski clear.
2. Get rid of skis, rucksack, etc.
3. Swim to stay on the surface.
4. If buried, cover your face with your hands.
5. Make a last big effort to clear an air space.

If you are buried, remember:

1. Don't panic.
2. Try to dig your way out.
3. Don't shout.

If you are a survivor in an avalanche:

1. Don't panic; check for further danger.
2. Mark the last point where buried companions were seen.
3. Make a quick search.
4. Make a thorough search (two hours is the critical time).
5. Send for help.
6. Use probing and dogs.

Avalanche Transceivers

Avalanche transceivers are electronic devices that can both transmit and receive a pulse signal. Skiers wear them close to the body and switch on to transmit for the duration of a ski tour. Should the group be avalanched and some of the party buried, the survivors switch to receive and then home in on the buried skiers, which can normally be done in a few minutes. Unless the buried skier is located within thirty minutes there is less than a fifty per cent chance of survival.

There are a number of different types of transceiver on sale in Europe and not all are compatible. Make sure all those in use in your party are of the same type. Practise search techniques regularly by burying one of the transceivers. Practice will greatly improve your speed and ability to locate a buried skier. Make sure that the batteries used are in good condition and of the type recommended by the manufacturers.

Avalanche transceivers can be hired from a number of ski clubs and specialist retail outlets or can be purchased for about one hundred pounds each (1987).

EQUIPMENT FOR MOUNTAIN SKI TOURING

Individual Mountain Equipment

1. Medium-sized rucksack with a hip belt and side straps for carrying skis.
2. A full protective suit of nylon or Gortex.
3. Bivi bag.
4. Map, compass and whistle.
5. Ice-axe, fitted with a rubber bung protector over the spike.
6. Crampons.
7. A small first-aid kit.
8. A headlamp.
9. Avalanche transceiver (optional).
10. A flask containing hot drink and food for the day.
11. Sunglasses.
12. Spare food.
13. Spare hat or Balaclava.
14. Spare gloves or mitts.
15. Spare sweater.
16. Spare stockings.

Mountain Ski Equipment

1. Mountain-type ski boot with Vibram-type sole, or similar.

2. Mountain skis with a full metal edge.
3. Robust 75mm (3in) Nordic binding fitted with a safety strap.
4. Strong alloy ski pole with full-sized basket.
5. Adhesive skins or wax.

Group Equipment

1. Large survival bag.
2. Lightweight snow shovel.

7 Ski Racing

Ski touring, as we have seen, can be arduous, challenging and exciting, particularly when carried out in isolated regions and over difficult mountain terrain, but it represents only one end of the varied cross-country skiing spectrum. Many skiers will prefer gentler recreational skiing, whilst others in whom the competitive instinct is strong will find that once they have gained a modicum of proficiency in the sport they will want to set their skills and their physical fitness to the test by competing against others on the racecourse. Just as cross-country skiing in general embraces a wide variety of allied activities, so the racing side of the sport produces a whole gamut of events, ensuring that each skier can find within the competitive programme the type of race that suits his personality and his abilities.

Fig 64   In racing, attention to detail is of vital importance. Here a competitor adds the final touches to the waxing of his skis shortly before the start of Germany's most famous citizens' race, the 65km König Ludwig Lauf.

Cross-country ski races fall into one of two categories. They are either individual start time trials against the clock, or they are mass start races with the first competitor across the finishing line the winner. Major international competitions such as the Winter Olympic Games, the World Championships, the World Cup and other races organised in accordance with the rules of the Fédération Internationale de Ski (FIS) all fall into the former category, whilst the vast majority of popular long-distance races are mass start events.

INDIVIDUAL START RACES
(*Fig 65*)

In individual start races each skier will normally start at a thirty-second interval from the competitor in front. Run in prepared tracks, the courses are normally set on forest tracks below the tree-line, with an equal amount of uphill, downhill and flat terrain included in the course. To ensure that the faster skiers always have a clear course, the competitor in front must clear the track whenever an overtaking skier calls for the right of way.

The standard racing distances for men are 15km (9$^1/_3$ miles), 30km (18$^2/_3$ miles) and 50km (31 miles) and for women 5km (3$^1/_{12}$ miles), 10km (6$^1/_5$ miles) and 20km (12$^2/_5$ miles), although there are moves afoot to increase the distances of the ladies' races in line with modern thinking and experience – there is ample evidence in many sports to dispel the old wives' tale that the 'weaker sex' are lacking in stamina. The standard relay events are 4 × 10km (6$^1/_5$ miles) for men and 4 × 5km (3$^1/_{10}$ miles) for women. The course setter's objective in all these events is to test every element of the racer's technical repertoire by making him constantly think ahead to the next variation in climb, descent or direction. The FIS lay down strict rules to govern the total amount of climb on the course, as well as the maximum length of any individual climb and the maximum

Race		HD	MC	MT
Men	10km (6$^1/_5$ miles)	200m (656ft)	100m (328ft)	300–450m (984–1,476ft)
	15km (9$^1/_3$ miles)	250m (820ft)	100m (328ft)	450–600m (1,476–1,968ft)
	30km (18$^2/_3$ miles)	250m (820ft)	100m (328ft)	900–1,200m (2,952–3,936ft)
	50km (31 miles)	250m (820ft)	100m (328ft)	1,000–1,500m (3,280–4,920ft)
Women	5km (3$^1/_{10}$ miles)	100m (328ft)	50m (164ft)	120–200m (393–656ft)
	10km (6$^1/_5$ miles)	150m (492ft)	75m (246ft)	250–400m (820–1,312ft)
	20km (12$^2/_5$ miles)	250m (820ft)	75m (246ft)	400–700m (1,312–2,296ft)

Notes
HD: Maximum difference in height between the lowest and highest points of a course.
MC: The maximum length of any single climb without a break of at least 200m.
MT: The maximum total climb of the course.

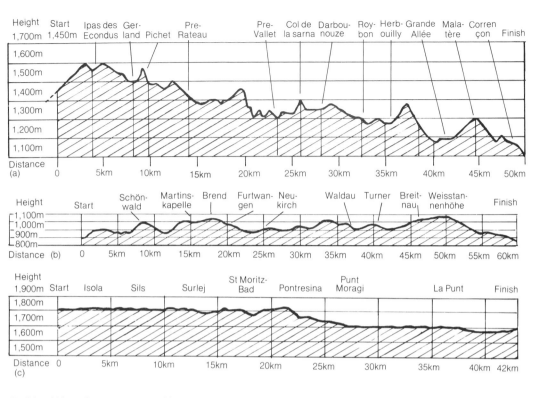

Fig 66 *Citizens' races vary considerably in their degree of difficulty as well as the length of their courses. Illustrated are the course profiles of three popular races: (a) the Traversée du Vercors, France, 50km; (b) the Black Forest Marathon, Germany, 60km; (c) the Engadin Skimarathon, Switzerland, 42km.*

differential between the lowest and highest points on the course. Although these rules are designed to limit the severity of the course, a glance at *Fig 65* will show that even when courses are set at the FIS minimum they can provide an extremely arduous physical and technical challenge.

CITIZENS' RACING

In parallel with these high intensity, single start time trials there exists a separate form of racing of at least equal popularity. It is known as citizens' racing, or tour racing in Scandinavia. The longest established of these events, such as the Holmenkoll-marsjen in Norway, the Vasaloppet in Sweden, and the Oulo-hiihto, the world's oldest ski race, which is held in Finland, go back to the early part of this century. Some – notably the Vasaloppet and the Birkebeiner-rennet – have their origins in their nation's history. For many years these long-distance events were skied annually by a handful of dedicated and experienced competitors. In the last few years of the 1960s and the early 1970s, however, there was a sudden boom in interest in citizens' racing, comparable to, but preceding, the boom in distance running on the roads that has also taken place in Europe and North America. Long-distance races started to attract huge crowds of participants, more than fifteen thousand in the case of the Vasaloppet and the Finlandia Hiihto, with similar figures taking part in the Foulée Blanche in France. The great attraction of these mass start events for the average skier is that whatever your level, there will always be others of similar ability in the field and hundreds, indeed thousands, of private battles are waged along the course, often by individuals who have never set eyes on one another until they met on the start line.

The World Loppet

In 1978 a notable event in the history of citizens' racing occurred when the organisers of nine of the world's leading long-distance races joined forces to form the World Loppet. This series of races consists of the major competition in each of the participating countries. Any skier may apply for a World Loppet passport in which each race features on a separate page. As each race is completed, the details on the page are filled in and the page is officially stamped; when all pages are complete, the skier is entitled to receive the World Loppet medallion, whether he has taken one year or a lifetime to achieve his aim. Since the original founding of the series, it has been enlarged by the addition of France's Transjurassienne in 1979 and the Sapporo International 50km (31 miles), in Japan, in 1986. With the inclusion of this last race, the rules have been amended slightly, so that it is now only necessary to complete ten of the eleven races to achieve the World Loppet medallion.

At the time of writing, the World Loppet consists of the events listed in *Fig 68*. The success of the World Loppet has been so

Fig 67   The World Loppet. In the centre, the coveted medallion, flanked by two passports, the one on the right showing that its owner has completed the Vasaloppet and the Engadin Skimarathon.

Dolomitenlauf	Lienz	Austria	60km (37$^{1}/_3$ miles)
Marcialonga	Moena-Cavalese	Italy	70km (43$^{1}/_2$ miles)
Konig Ludwig Lauf	Oberammergau	West Germany	65km (40$^{1}/_2$ miles)
Transjurassienne	Lamoura-Mouthe	France	79km (49 miles)
Finlandia Hiihto	Hameenlinna-Lahti	Finland	75km (46$^{1}/_2$ miles)
Gatineau 55	Hull, Quebec	Canada	55km (34 miles)
Vasaloppet	Salen-Mora	Sweden	89km (55$^{1}/_3$ miles)
American Birkebeiner	Hayward, Wisconsin	USA	55km (34 miles)
Sapporo 50	Sapporo	Japan	50km (31 miles)
Engadin Skimarathon	Maloja-Zuoz	Switzerland	42km (26 miles)
Birkebeiner-rennet *	Rena-Lillehammer	Norway	55km (34 miles)

* The direction of this race is changed every alternate year.

Fig 68   Events included in the World Loppet.

great that many other Citizens' Racing Leagues have sprung up. The Alpentris can be accomplished by completing any three of the Dolomitenlauf, Marcialonga, König Ludwig Lauf, Transjurassienne and Engadin Skimarathon in any one year; the Euroloppet by finishing in three races out of the Dolomitenlauf, Marcialonga, König Ludwig Lauf, Finlandia and Vasaloppet, with the proviso that one race at least must be in Scandinavia and one in the Alps. Germany now has its Deutschland Loppet and Austria and Switzerland their own national series. The USA has the Great American Ski Chase, with races spread from New England to the Rockies and California and Canada plans to introduce a similar competition in the 1986–87 season. France has perhaps the best developed series of all, with a French Long Distance Challenge, in 'A' and 'B' sections, comprising between them no fewer than twenty-one races. Even Belgium has its own four-race series in the Ardennes, whilst in 1987 Sweden initiated its 'Classic Triss', embracing the Vasaloppet, Norrbarke Skimarathon and Engelbrektsloppet.

Citizens' races now exist in their hundreds throughout Central Europe, North America and Scandinavia and they provide the perfect opportunity for the competent skier to test his skills against others of similar background. Besides those already mentioned, the names of intriguing races roll off the tongue: the Nordfest in Murmansk, the Lavaloppet in Iceland, the Isergebirgslauf in Czechoslovakia, the Marcha Beret in Spain or – for the real adventurer – any one of a number of races in Australia, which surprisingly boasts a bigger snow area than Switzerland. One point which facilitates planning to take part in those races is that they are normally held on the same day each year, the Dolomitenlauf, for example, taking place on the penultimate Sunday in January, the König Ludwig Lauf on the first Sunday in February and the Engadin Skimarathon on the second Sunday in March.

Most of the best-known citizens' races are long-distance or marathon events, but there is a host of other races ranging in length from only a handful of kilometres upwards, whilst many of the tourist resorts hold weekly races aimed at attracting the more energetic of their visitors. Nor is the older skier overlooked; there is a growing programme of masters' races aimed at veteran skiers, with an annual Masters' World Cup meeting offering competition in five year age brackets from thirty to seventy plus.

One citizens' race deserves a special mention – the Vasaloppet. It is neither the most difficult nor the most attractive of the World Loppet courses, but the question asked of all citizen racers by their co-competitors is still 'Have you skied the Vasa?'.

Perhaps it is its age and historical background which give it such prestige that entries close (at 15,000 competitors) on the same day that they open, and thousands of disappointed would-be competitors are consigned to the Oppet Spar (or 'open course'), which permits them to ski the course and receive a certificate showing the time taken during the week preceding the race itself.

Fig 69   The Vasaloppet is the most prestigious of all long-distance ski races. Each year a limited number of places in the start list is reserved for British competitors, but as this picture demonstrates, more than 10,000 other racers may have priority on the starting line.

Championships for British Skiers

For British skiers the major race meeting of the season is the British Championships, a ten-day meeting in late January incorporating both cross-country and biathlon events and organised in conjunction with the Army and Inter-Services Championships. These championships are always held in Europe and for a number of years have taken place at Zwiesel, a small resort on the German/Czechoslovakian border, set amidst the hills of the Bayerischer Wald which provide an excellent range of varied tracks to test the abilities of skiers of all levels. From these championships selected skiers go on to represent their country at the World Championships and Winter Olympic Games, in World Cup and Alpen Cup races, and in the Lowlanders' Championships, a competition open only to those countries that are not normally blessed with reliable skiing conditions.

The United Kingdom Cross-country Championships held in Aviemore in February attracts up to four hundred competitors each year, making it Britain's

Fig 70   For the children of this Austrian village, a World Cup race means a welcome day off school.

*Fig 71   Team officials cluster around the results board on which each
competitor's time is displayed within a few seconds of his
crossing the finishing line.*

biggest ski event. Apart from attracting the best of British skiers, it includes races for all ages and abilities. Scotland also offers a varied and increasing racing programme from January through to early May. Glen Isla is developing a considerable programme; the facilities at Clashindarroch Forest near Huntly are being improved each year by the Forestry Commission and are the venue for the Army (UK) Championships which are open to all-comers; Highland Guides meanwhile hold late season meetings at high level on the Cairngorms. The snow in England is less predictable, but races have been held with varying degrees of success in the Yorkshire Dales.

SKATING IN COMPETITION

In the past few years, a major controversy – the skating question – has plagued race organisers and competitors alike. The introduction of single-sided skating to the racing world is attributed to the Finn Pauli Siitonen, one of the most successful of all citizens' racers, who took a centuries-old technique and adapted it to the demands of long-distance racing. The Americans, led by Olympic silver medallist Bill Koch, extended the use of skating to World Cup events, and the advantages in speed of both single and double-sided skating became so obvious that by the time of the 1985 World Championships, skaters were winning all the medals to the total exclusion of those practising the traditional techniques, such as two-phase and double pole. The FIS was forced to react to the situation and, as a result, from the 1985–86 season onwards, international races must be designated as being conducted in either the free technique (skating) or classical modes. At major championships the races are divided evenly between the two styles.

These two differing styles have necessi-

tated different methods of preparing the racing tracks. Classical tracks are now prepared with one single track set in the centre of the course, while free-style courses are pisted to a width of 3.5m (11ft 5in), but have a single track set to one side following the best skiing line. It is important to remember that whilst the vast majority of racers will be skating the whole course, the race is termed 'free technique' and classical methods of progression may still be used, hence the need for the single track.

The impact of skating on citizens' racing is almost as great and the problem has yet to be properly resolved. The proponents of skating contend that racers should be

Fig 72   Skating is now accepted as a racing technique in its own right. Norway's World Championship relay gold medallist Ove Aunli skates away from the start in a World Cup race.

competing effectively, that skaters create bottle-necks in narrow sections of the course and in the starting area, and that widespread use of skating will create an ever widening gulf between the racer and the recreational skier. Various solutions to the problem have been sought, ranging from separate races for skaters and classical skiers, to parallel tracks with skaters on one side of the course and classical skiers on the other. Some events – notably the Vasaloppet – have banned any form of skating during the race while the 1986–87 season has seen the formation of a World Grand Prix of Classical Cross-country Skiers, comprising the races listed in *Fig 74*.

Only time will tell whether this is the start of a split in popular skiing similar to the two-technique concept already developed for international competition, or whether some form of accord between the two styles will yet be reached.

Fig 73   Finland's Ari Hynninen skates a downhill section of the course with two other competitors in hot pursuit.

permitted to use the fastest possible means to get from start to finish. Its opponents claim that skating destroys the tracks, preventing 'classical' skiers from

SKI-ORIENTEERING

One further form of skiing competition, although not perhaps falling strictly within the definition of ski racing, is ski-orienteering, or Ski-O, as it is popularly known.

Giant's Ridge International Classic Marathon	USA	30km (18²/₃ miles)
Pustertaler Skimarathon	Italy	42km (26 miles)
Marcha Beret	Spain	42km (26 miles)
Internationaler Deutscher Skimarathon in Hirschau	West Germany	42km (26 miles)
Engelbrektsloppet	Sweden	60km (37¹/₃ miles)
Internationaler Tiroler Koasalauf	Austria	42/72km (26/44²/₃ miles)
Einsiedler Volkslauf	Switzerland	30km (18²/₃ miles)
Soisalen Hiihto	Finland	65km (40¹/₂ miles)

Fig 74   Events included in the World Grand Prix of Cross-country Skiers.

NORDIC INSTRUCTION WEEK — 3rd-9th January

Transport arrangements

We will be travelling in two minibuses, with one trailer, and cars, leaving from the ski garage off George Square at 2pm on Sunday 3rd January, ie please be there shortly after 1.30pm so that we can actually leave at 2pm.

On the return journey we will be leaving after a full day's skiing on Saturday 9th January, arriving back in Edinburgh by about 9pm.

Fig 76   . . . as long as they are fit and young at heart.

As the name suggests it is similar in concept to orienteering on foot, but with the limitation that the skier can rarely cut across country on a direct bearing, but must follow established tracks. Apart from the contour features and trees, most other identifiable landmarks may be covered by snow and it is route choice, allied to skiing ability, that is the critical factor. Ski-O is particularly popular in Scandinavia, but is becoming increasingly widely practised in other countries, with the 1986 World Championships being held in Bulgaria. British teams have taken part in these and previous World Championships with some success, although the opportunities to practise in Britain have until now been very limited. There are indications, however, that more frequent Ski-O events may be held in Scotland in coming years, although unreliable snow conditions have so far thwarted plans to mount a regular Ski-O programme south of the border.

CONCLUSIONS

The possibilities for racing on skis are endless and this chapter has by no means exhausted the available options. Biathlon is dealt with separately in Chapter 8, but there are many other races of individual character, such as the Pinzolo 24-hour race and its imitators, and the Immenstadt Cross-country race – a mixture of straight cross-country, ski mountaineering and downhill. Competition is healthy and many valuable lessons are learned on the race-course that might never be driven home when skiing at a more leisurely pace. Here we have suggested some of the choices that are open to you as a would-be competitor. Our final thought to those of you who would like to take part, but are reticent about entering your first race in case the opposition is too strong is: take the plunge! In citizens' racing, certainly, it is participation that is important. Its philosophy is summed up in the twin mottoes of the Dolomitenlauf: *'Jeder ein sieger über sich selbst. Dabei sein ist alles'*. (Everyone a victor over himself. Taking part is all-important).

8 Biathlon

Much of the success of British skiers in international competitions in recent years has been gained in biathlon, a sport which combines cross-country skiing and shooting and which has a growing number of devotees throughout the world. Its appeal lies not just in the combination of two different sports, but in the challenge of dovetailing their apparently incompatible requirements to achieve success.

Competitive cross-country skiing demands all-out effort, resulting in a high pulse-rate, heavy breathing and a gradual diminution of the oxygen supply which, as fatigue increases and the end of the race draws near, may result in slight unsteadiness, impaired judgement and blurred vision. All these things are anathema to the rifleman who requires a calm, steady, unhurried approach to his task, with his mind and

Fig 77 *A biathlon race at the British Championships. Rifle on back, a competitor skates away from the range with another racer in close pursuit.*

vision clear and his powers of concentration and judgement totally unaffected by outside events.

BASIC FORMAT

The basic format of any biathlon race is for the competitor to ski a circuit carrying his rifle on his back, enter the 50-metre (162ft 6in) range, fire five rounds in the prone or standing position at a falling target and then ski on again. The number of times he is required to carry out a shooting practice varies with the length of the race. The two normal races in international competition are the 10km ($6^1/_5$ miles) sprint race and the 20km ($12^2/_5$ miles). In the former, competitors fire one five-round practice prone and one five-round practice standing, and must ski once round a 150-metre (487ft 6in) penalty loop, situated near the exit to the range, for every shot they miss. In the longer race, competitors fire four range practices, two lying and two standing, but instead of skiing a penalty loop, they have one minute added to their overall time for each target they fail to hit. The penalties for poor shooting in the longer race are therefore very severe and international biathletes will be looking for at least four clear hits on each practice.

Fig 78   Skiing the penalty loop: once round the circuit for every target missed.

The relay race is 4 × 7.5km (4 ×4²/₃ miles), and the rules are in essence identical to those for the 10km (6¹/₅ miles) sprint. Singularly, biathlon competition is controlled not by the FIS but by the UIPMB (Union International de Pentathlon Moderne et Biathlon) who hold their own World Cup and World Championships quite separate from those organised by the FIS for Nordic skiing.

HISTORY

Not surprisingly, involvement in biathlon has, since its early beginnings and until recently, been very largely the province of the military. By the early years of the eighteenth century, skiing was being recognised as a military pursuit and special regiments were being formed. The first ski regiment was formed in 1733 in Trondheim, Norway, and the regimental

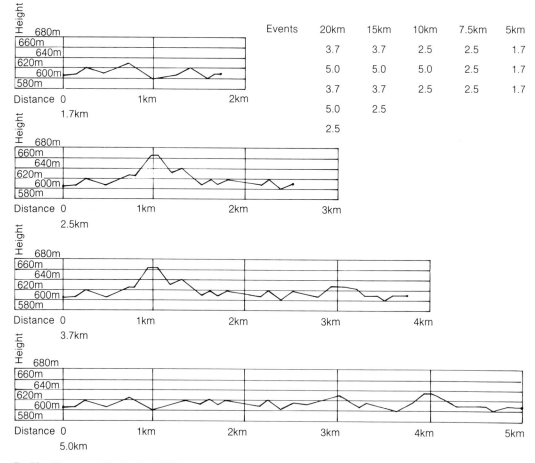

Events	20km	15km	10km	7.5km	5km
	3.7	3.7	2.5	2.5	1.7
	5.0	5.0	5.0	2.5	1.7
	3.7	3.7	2.5	2.5	1.7
	5.0	2.5			
	2.5				

Fig 79 Course profiles for the 1986 World Biathlon Championships. As with straight cross-country races, the courses should in principle be one-third flat, one-third uphill and one-third downhill. No concessions are made for the fact that the competitor must carry his rifle on his back throughout the race.

regulations required training in both skiing techniques and marksmanship. The first mention of what we would now call biathlon comes in a Norwegian decree of 1767:

'The award in the art of skiing is as follows: first class – two awards of 20 talers for those who ski at full speed on a moderate hill and shoot their weapon to hit a suitably placed target at a distance of 40–50 paces.'

In Germany too 'ski soldiers' were active as long ago as the late eighteenth century and the military authorities put up monetary awards for those 'who can ski 2.5km on the flat, in full uniform, with shouldered rifle, in less than fifteen minutes'. Even in those days, however, it was not all military, and the Trysil Shooting and Skiing Club, founded in Norway in 1861, lays claim, with the Kiandra Club in Australia, to being the oldest ski club in the world.

There were two major differences between the ski shooting of the nineteenth and early twentieth centuries and biathlon as we know it today. In those early competitions, the targets were not placed at a fixed distance from the firing point but would suddenly appear at varying distances down the range. The competitor would apply his military or hunting skills in judging the distance to the target and adjusting his aim or his sights before firing. The rifles used were, of course, full-bore, and consequently were heavier to carry and less accurate than the small-bore weapons that are now in use.

Today, the military influence, while still strong, is diminishing somewhat as the appeal of the sport grows. Biathlon became an Olympic event in 1960 at the Squaw Valley, USA Winter Olympics, and

there are now World Championships for juniors as well as for senior men and unofficial World Championships for ladies, although presently these are – as for all ladies' races – held at shorter distances than those over which the men race. Since ladies' biathlon is still in the throes of development and has not yet attracted mass participation from the Scandinavians, it would appear that biathlon provides an ideal opportunity for skiers seeking to attain international status in competition to make their mark.

COMPETITION TODAY

Equipment

The equipment used in biathlon is in essence the same as that used for competitive cross-country skiing, with the addition, of course, of the rifle. Because all biathlon races are free-style, which means that the courses are skated by all the leading competitors, the skis used are shorter than would be the case for classical cross-country races, and the poles are longer, exactly as would be the case in a free-style cross-country race. Clothing is identical, but all competitors are required to carry their rifle with them throughout the competition.

These rifles were originally full-bore, but the change in 1978 to small-bore weapons and 50-metre (162ft 6in) ranges greatly increased biathlon's spectator appeal. The biathlon rifle is a .22 calibre weapon specifically designed for biathlon competition. The most popular make is undoubtedly the West German Anschutz model, but other weapons, from Finland and elsewhere, are also widely used in competition. The rifle is flat-sided, allowing

Fig 80   The rifle must be carried on the back throughout the race.

it to be carried comfortably on the back by means of a carrying harness, and the butt is recessed to take four five-round magazines for loading at each range practice. Hinged covers to keep the snow off the fore and rear sights complete the distinctive features of the weapon.

Summer Variations

The UIPMB is currently promoting summer biathlon as a means of popularising the sport and of providing off-season training for the winter season. The essential philosophy of the sport is the same as for winter biathlon, except that the competitor substitutes cross-country running for the skiing phases of the race. Some competitions have also been run in which roller skiing has been used to take the place of the skiing elements, but this is not the general pattern. It frequently happens in summer biathlon events that the rifle is not carried by the competitor, but is left on the firing point. This gives far more people the opportunity to compete, as there is no necessity for one rifle for each competitor, and 'come and try it' events can be held to broaden interest and participation in the sport.

The need for a safe rifle range remains one of the limiting factors in organising a biathlon competition, but a leading firm of British gunsmiths is working on the development of an air rifle with a muzzle velocity sufficient to carry with accuracy down a 50-metre (162ft 6in) range, but with a safety zone behind the range far smaller than that needed for the conventional .22 calibre weapon. The production of such a rifle could result in a dramatic increase both in the incidence of summer biathlon races and the number of competitors taking part in the sport.

THE FUTURE

Of all the Nordic skiing events, the biathlon – apart perhaps from the head-to-head competition of the cross-country relays – is surely the event with the greatest spectator appeal. Each competitor entering the range shoots at five black targets. Each good shot knocks down the black disc and brings a white disc up in its place, giving the spectator an immediate visual picture of the effectiveness of the shooting. The psychological boost of 'five whites' for the competitor is also evident as he slings his rifle on his back, picks up his poles and

*Fig 81   The five white discs on the target in Lane 20 show that the com-
petitor has had a clear round. The dark square to the right of the
stand is not a missed target - it is a marker to indicate that the
target is set for firing in the standing position.*

races away from the range.

It is a sad fact that at present few people outside the Armed Forces have the opportunity to try biathlon. However, the development of summer biathlon and the building of projected biathlon ranges in Scotland should mean that within the next few years many more young people will have the chance to participate in this demanding, exacting and rewarding offshoot of cross-country skiing.

9 Fitness and Training

At any level, cross-country skiing demands above-average physical fitness. At the peak of Olympic or World Championship racing, this is an obvious statement, since the physiological requirements placed upon the competitor are at least as great as those in any other sport. However, this is also just as true for the family tourer. Skiing fluently up a hill without panting and gasping for breath is a much more pleasur-able experience than plodding up the same hill stopping every few metres to take a break to recover from the exhaustion. A keen cross-country skier will put many kilometres behind him during a day's outing and to do this he must develop stamina and aerobic fitness to match his technical skill.

PREPARATION

The acquisition of fitness is not something that can wait until the start of the ski season, nor even until the autumn when next season's programme is being planned. It can only be acquired and main-tained by following a life-style that is geared to physical activity, whether this be the planned training programme of the competitive athlete or merely the active participation in regular exercise that may be undertaken by the recreational or family skier.

Cross-country skiing is a whole-body sport, using arms and legs in unison as well as placing demands on the strength, stamina and suppleness of all the other major muscle groups. All exercise is therefore beneficial to skiing in some way, and even if you are an office worker com-muting daily to London from your home in the suburbs or beyond, you will find that there are many ways in which you can enhance your general fitness levels. Fitness starts with life-style and with attitudes, and it entails a positive dis-sociation from some of the trappings of modern civilisation, or more accurately of mechanisation. Public Enemy Number One in the fitness stakes is the motor car, whilst Public Enemy Number Two is the junk food diet.

Good health and fitness go hand in hand and a wholesome, active, outdoor life-style is a good basis from which to begin. It will not, however, be enough on its own to develop the level of fitness that the long-distance skier requires. When Fausto Coppi, the great Italian racing cyclist of the 1950s, was asked for three pieces of advice that he would give to a young cyclist, he replied: 'One, ride a bike; two, ride a bike; three, ride a bike', The same advice holds true for skiing. The best training for skiing is undoubtedly to get out on skis for as often and as long as you can, since this improves technique, thereby reducing energy wastage through inef-ficient muscular actions, whilst developing and exercising the muscle groups specifi-cally utilised in cross-country skiing. However, even in lowland and snow-free countries such as the southern part of Britain, there are many activities that can be practised which will also exercise these very muscle groups, improve your aerobic capacity, develop balance and, in some cases, actually enable skiing techniques to be polished and perfected.

FITNESS TRAINING

Probably the most common form of fitness training in the western world at present is running, or jogging as it is now increasingly known in its non-competitive form. Running is a basic form of aerobic fitness training for all endurance sports and whilst it has no specific relationship to the mechanics of cross-country skiing, it is extremely beneficial in its development of the cardio-vascular system (the heart and lungs). For the casual skier, regular runs at a steady pace will probably be enough to raise the fitness level to a point at which physical effort can be sustained without discomfort, remembering the principle that 'little and often' is better than a lot of exercise every now and again. However, the more aggressive or competitive skier will want to undertake a more intensive training programme.

Programme

The secret of any successful training programme is to find the right blend of quantity and quality. Long, slow runs undoubtedly develop stamina but it is a mistake to reckon the amount of training carried out simply on the basis of the number of miles run. To realise your full potential, a significant amount of high-quality speed work must be included in the programme. Since it is clear that high speeds can only be maintained for short distances, the basic format of a speed session is to run a fast stretch, rest, then repeat, but there are many different ways in which this package can be presented and the method chosen may depend as much on your personality as on the environment in which you are training.

Fartlek

The general theme of any off-season fitness training programme should be related as closely as possible to cross-country skiing. You should therefore run over natural country, preferably rolling woodland, where both the terrain and the environment will be similar to that encountered during the winter, and will therefore provide you with both physical and mental links to your objectives. A very effective form of training is fartlek (a Swedish word meaning speed-play), in which the pace varies according to the nature of the terrain. Short, fast bursts of running may be interspersed with longer stretches at medium pace, with long or short recoveries, and possibly even walking on short, sharp uphills.

Interval Training

For city-dwellers, or others who find it hard to train in natural surroundings, interval training can be substituted or used in addition to fartlek. This will consist of a series of repeated fast runs with stretches of jogging to enable partial recovery between each. The fast stretches, which should be in the 200–1,000m (216–1,083 yds) range, could be run on a track, but any other convenient method of measurement, such as the lamp-posts down the street, can be used equally well.

Hill Running

Hill running is another variant on the theme of repetitive fast bursts. Research in the USSR and Eastern Europe has shown that greater benefits are gained from repeated fast runs on a 200-metre (216yds) hill than from fewer, longer runs on a hill of equal steepness. Hill running can therefore be carried out effectively in only moderately undulating terrain.

Walking

Hiking and hill walking provide some of the benefits of running and are possible alternatives to long runs as a means of developing stamina. Anyone taking part in mountain touring or in citizens' races, in which you may have to spend as long as nine or ten hours on your skis, can derive considerable benefit from a regimen of long walks over arduous terrain. Hiking, by itself, will not provide a wide range of physical benefits and must be used in concert with other activities aligned to speed and suppleness if an all-round physical improvement is to be achieved. Hiking and hill running, as we shall see later, can also be done with poles. There are some coaches who advocate that skiers take their poles with them whenever they set out for any form of run or hike, and there is certainly much to recommend this approach.

Cycling

Many good skiers prefer cycling to running and the two activities give very similar aerobic benefits whilst sharing the advantage that they can be carried out from your own front door. Cycling strengthens and develops the quadriceps - the muscles in

the top of the thigh - and is therefore a particularly useful training medium for skiers who make regular use of the skating techniques. It may also be useful in improving balance, a quality it shares with rowing and particularly canoeing, which are excellent activities for the development of the upper body. The need to exercise the arms becomes evident when it is realised that around about forty per cent of the forward momentum in cross-country skiing certainly at racing level, is derived from the thrust on the poles.

Swimming

Another widely practised activity is swimming, which has traditionally been thought to be incompatible with dry-land activities, although modern pentathletes who must be equally proficient at swimming and running, and triathletes who do both activities on the same day, suggest that this is an outdated concept. Swimming is certainly an excellent method of continuing to exercise whilst suffering from the type of muscle or leg injury which is aggravated by jarring contact with the ground. Such injuries respond well to the supporting effect of water, which also helps to relax tired and aching muscles.

Roller Skiing (Figs 82 & 83)

The activities above are all geared to general fitness and are readily accessible to most people. Activities with a specific relationship to cross-country may be of greater value, but are possibly harder to undertake regularly. Roller skiing is undoubtedly the most realistic of these activities and the one practised the most widely in both Scandinavian and Alpine countries, but it does require traffic-free

Fig 82   Roller skiing is a training activity with specific relationship to cross-country skiing, providing both technique and fitness training.

roads if it is to be carried out safely, and smooth tarmac if techniques are to be polished and improved. Dedicated cycle tracks, such as the Eastway Cycle Circuit at Lee Valley in East London, where the English Ski Council Roller Skiing Championships have been held several times, make ideal venues for training and competition, as do traffic-free tarmac paths in parks. Battersea Park (London), Sefton Park (Liverpool) and Bellahouston Park (Glasgow) have all staged successful roller ski race meetings. In Europe, roller skiing has developed into a major summer sport, some of whose adherents, particularly in countries like Holland, may rarely have skied on snow. Roller skis are now avail-able from all major stockists of cross-country equipment in the United Kingdom, and you are no longer regarded as an eccentric if seen poling your way along a country road on a quiet training spin.

Downhill Training (Fig 84)

Artificial downhill slopes can be exploited profitably using either Alpine or Nordic equipment. For many cross-country skiers, downhill techniques are their main weakness and confidence on downhills can only be gained by spending as much time as possible skiing downhill. The beginner is best advised to use Alpine equipment which gives greater stability and control,

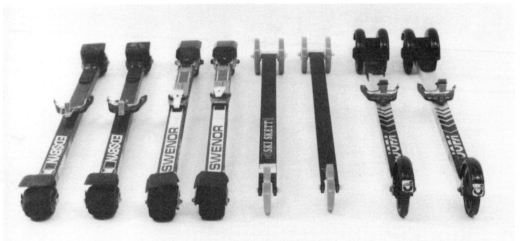

Fig 83   Numerous models of roller ski are now available. The main
differentiation in type is between three-wheeled roller skis (the
two pairs on the right) and the two pairs on the left which have
single 'barrel' wheels front and back.

but once confidence has been established, techniques can be practised equally well using conventional cross-country skis. Make sure you do not take your best skis, as plastic surfaces play havoc with the soles of the skis, and wear gloves, watching out for your thumbs in the event of a fall; broken thumbs are easily sustained in the event of a fall on artificial matting.

Arm Strengthening (Fig 85)

Some firms have developed equipment aimed at specific training in the environment of a gymnasium. One of the best known of these gadgets is the Exer-Genie, an expensive device designed to simulate the co-ordinated arm and leg movements used in the two-phase or diagonal stride. A cheaper, but equally effective alternative, used for years by the Scandinavians, is an

old bicycle inner tube cut to make one long strip and anchored to a wall or a tree at the middle, at about eye level. The skier faces the point at which the rubber is anchored and pulls down alternately on each end of the inner tube to simulate the poling action. By altering the distance at which the exerciser stands away from the wall, the tension can be adjusted to give harder or weaker resistance in accordance with the wishes and capabilities of the user.

Hill Bounding (Fig 86)

Back in the fresh air, hill bounding with poles trains the upper body as well as the lungs and heart. The exercise is essential for the serious skier, but should be tackled only in moderation by those who are not fully fit, as it can place considerable physiological demands on the body. A moderate hill is needed, preferably one long enough to accommodate a run of not

Fig 84 Artificial ski slopes are ideal places for the cross-country skier to practise his downhill techniques during the summer season. Nordic equipment may be used, but greater confidence will be gained by using the more responsive Alpine boots and skis.

Fig 85 The simulated poling exercise can be used either on its own or in conjunction with other activities as part of an outdoor circuit.

Fig 86   Strength training does not demand access to a gymnasium or to sophisticated weight-training equipment. Nature provides us with a ready supply of aids to the training programme. This sizeable log makes a convenient barbell.

less than sixty strides. A good grass or pine needle surface is ideal, but if this cannot be found, at least try to avoid a surface with too many ruts, as these can easily cause ankle injury. Bound up the hill with long strides, landing on the heel and simulating the leg action used in skiing uphill. At the same time, drive hard on the poles. A high bound on each stride is essential, as a low, quick stride will not permit a proper co-ordinated thrust with the poles. If a long hill bounding session proves too monotonous, try including it in a session of circuit training. A specimen circuit might follow a mile-long undulating path through the woods. Run as many laps of the circuit as possible, stopping at four roughly equal points on each lap for half a dozen hill bounding runs, for some weight-lifting repetitions with a convenient log, for some leg or stomach exercises and for a hundred simulated poling actions using a cycle tyre and tree in the way described above.

Gymnasium Work

For those of you who have little opportunity to get out in the fresh air or who want to supplement your outdoor activity with some gymnasium work, a number of very beneficial possibilities exist. The multi-gym will exercise and strengthen all parts of the body, depending on the exercise performed. Weight-training will similarly produce great gains in strength, whilst cycling and rowing machines will respectively improve the efficiency of the legs and arms.

Circuit training, which can be carried out effectively indoors as well as outside, is another excellent form of all-round fitness training. However, do not launch into any weight-training or gymnasium work unless you already have some experience or are able to call on the assistance of an experienced lifter or qualified coach. Incorrect techniques can lead to serious injury. In addition, all active exercise should be preceded by a short programme of stretching exercises which will loosen the body from head to toe before the serious work of training begins. Stretching is almost equally important *after* each training session. Five to ten minutes of static stretching, holding each stretched position for fifteen to thirty seconds should be carried out. For the competitive skier this is essential, but even for the casual

tourer, gentle stretching and exercising will go a long way towards eliminating the feelings of stiffness and soreness that so often follow the first long day on skis.

ASSESSING PROGRESS

If you are serious about fitness training, you will want to keep a daily diary of what you have done. An effective method of keeping track is to allot points for each session according to the nature and amount of work done. Work on the basis of three points a kilometre for running, two points a kilometre for roller skiing, canoeing, orienteering or circuit training and one

Fig 87   Stretching is an essential pre- and
post-training activity.

Fig 88   Start at the top of the body and work
right down to the toes.

point a kilometre for walking or cycling. The points allotted to any activity may, however, vary from these suggestions to reflect your own abilities. If you are a good canoeist, but a slow jogger, for instance, you will find you can take more out of yourself in the canoe and will therefore score more points in that activity. In most sports it is necessary to reach a certain level of skill before you can derive maximum aerobic value from the training. You must be honest with yourself and devise a personal points score that tells you how much work you have actually done.

Having worked out a comparative points table, a target must then be set, for example 80 points a week to start with. Every effort should be made to keep to this target and shortfalls one week must be made up the next. As fitness increases, the points target can be gradually increased until the maximum level is reached which is compatible with your life-style. As an indication of what can be achieved, an international competitor will probably score well over 480 points a week and a good club representative 360 plus. However, 80 points or so will achieve a very fair level of fitness, whilst most people regularly scoring over 160 points would consider themselves to be very fit.

SEASONAL PLANNING

It must always be remembered that fitness training is an ongoing, year-round activity. There is an old adage that skiers are made in the summer, polished in the autumn and sent out to show their paces in the winter. It is certainly true that last-minute rushes to achieve fitness are often counter-productive, leaving the skier either exhausted or injured. Work done in the winter can never make up for training missed between June and September. For the serious skier, the training year can be conveniently broken into four parts: April–May, the recuperation period; June–September, the stamina-building period; October–November, the speeding-up period; and December–March, the racing season. In practice, of course, the divisions are not this clear cut, and the various parts of the year run into one another, but the principle holds good of an easy recovery period to follow a season of heavy racing, leading into an increasingly heavy build-up, with the emphasis on stamina interspersed with shorter, sharper speed sessions. As the year progresses, the speed sessions become more frequent and more intensive until the racing season is under way and training tails off as the skier reserves his energies for the competitions.

SUMMARY

The amount and type of training that you will do is entirely related to such factors as your age, ambitions and the type of skiing that you propose to undertake. To see how you rate in the fitness stakes, take your pulse daily. First thing in the morning is a good time, when your heart is rested and is not having to cope with digestion, exercise or stress. Seventy-two beats per minute is normal; a fit sportsman should certainly be in the low fifties, whilst the very fit have been known to go below forty. How do you rate?

Fitness and training are subjects about which many books have been written and this chapter has merely outlined general suggestions. If you are ambitious, you will need to seek a good coach and to make an in-depth study of your requirements. If you are a weekend skier, by contrast, you may be content with a more modest programme. Either way, regular exercise throughout the year is the basis for success and enjoyment, not only when the snow is on the ground, but throughout your daily life. There is no truer saying than that a fit skier is a happy skier.

CONCLUSION

As we noted in the beginning, cross-country skiing covers a vast spectrum of activity, which is constantly changing as equipment and techniques seek to keep abreast of new materials and ideas. Keeping up with the latest state of the art is difficult for those of us who live in snow-free countries. Reading is a start, and hopefully this book will have provided a base on which to build, but the best way to increase your knowledge is to seek and take every opportunity to talk with more experienced skiers. Next time you go on a skiing holiday, go down to your hotel's basement waxing room in the evening. Watch the experts wax their skis; listen to them; talk to them. Then try their ideas out for yourself. As your knowledge increases, so will your level of performance, and so – above all – will your enjoyment. Happy skiing!

Further Reading

Barton, Bob and Wright, Blyth *A Chance in a Million*, The Scottish Mountaineering Trust (1985).

Cliff, Peter *Mountain Navigation*, Peter Cliff (1978).

Langmuir, Eric *Mountaincraft and Leadership*, The Scottish Sports Council (1984).

Useful Addresses

**The British Association of
Ski Instructors**
Aviemore,
Inverness-shire.

The British Ski Federation
118 Eaton Square,
London.

The Fédération Internationale de Ski
Worbstrasse 210
CH 3073 Gümlingen bei Berne,
Switzerland.

The English Ski Council
Area Library Building,
The Precinct,
Halesowen,
West Midlands.

The Scottish National Ski Council
18 Ainslie Place,
Edinburgh.

The Ski Council of Wales
Castledale House,
Welsh Street,
Chepstow,
Gwent.

The Ulster Ski Council
43 Ballymaconoll Road,
Bangor,
Northern Ireland.

Index

Crowood Sports Books

* **Badminton-**The Skills of the Game — *Peter Roper*
  Basketball-The Skills of the Game — *Paul Stimpson*
* **Canoeing-**Skills and Techniques — *Neil Shave*
* **The Skills of Cricket** — *Keith Andrew*
  Endurance Running — *Norman Brook*
* **Fitness for Sport** — *Rex Hazeldine*
* **Golf-**The Skills of the Game — *John Stirling*
  Hockey-The Skills of the Game — *John Cadman*
  Judo-Skills and Techniques — *Tony Reay*
  Jumping — *Malcolm Arnold*
  Rugby Union-The Skills of the Game — *Barrie Corless*
  Skiing-Developing Your Skill — *John Shedden*
  Cross-Country Skiing — *Paddy Field and Tim Walker*
  Sprinting and Hurdling — *Peter Warden*
  Squash-The Skills of the Game — *Ian McKenzie*
  Swimming — *John Verrier*
  Table Tennis-The Skills of the Game — *Gordon Steggall*
  Tennis-The Skills of the Game — *Charles Applewhaite and Bill Moss*
  Throwing — *Max Jones*
  Volleyball-The Skills of the Game — *Keith Nicholls*
  Windsurfing-Improving Techniques — *Ben Oakley*

* Also available in paperback

Further details of titles available or in preparation can be obtained from the publishers.